# Contents

KU-112-633

## Maps

## Walks and Tours

## Features

# Introduction

China is one of the world's most fascinating countries. Long hidden behind the impenetrable screen of its 'Bamboo Curtain', it is now open to the outside world. The incentive, and the reward, for a visitor is to 'catch' the country before too much change robs it of its mystery.

Universally known symbol of China – the Great Wall

Travelling through China is bound to be an unforgettable experience. The country has the largest population on earth, a 5,000-year-old culture, a language spoken by one-fifth of humanity, and a deep desire to be counted among the ranks of the advanced nations. Despite this, China makes few concessions (and often little sense) to foreign visitors.

Most visitors, travelling on tours with all the details organised – even down to the souvenirs they buy – may come away with a rose-tinted view of the country. They will see spectacular sights, stay at fine hotels and eat good food. Other travellers, who resolutely avoid the protective cocoon of an organised tour, may take a more jaundiced view, having had to fight, plead and bribe their way around the country, and stay in some pretty down-at-heel hotels.

The world's largest population dwells in China

Fascinating as China undoubtedly is, it is also a big and crowded place. This aspect of the country contrasts with breath-taking scenes of natural and man-made beauty. Unfortunately, many of China's finest sights have been swamped by crass commercialism. Only a few retain some of that intangible aura suggested by names that conjure up visions of misty rice-paper paintings and delicate poetry.

## Changed Times

This is partly due to the astonishing turmoil that China has experienced in the last half century. Change sometimes seems to be the only constant. Most recently, China has been propelled by a booming economy and a sense of horizons opening up – horizons that might be closed again by a shift in the political winds, although no-one knows what the awakening giant will do with its new powers. Given a stable political background, China will undoubtedly go a long way. Travelling in China gives us a chance to try to unravel some of the strands in the Chinese puzzle, and have some fun along the way.

China

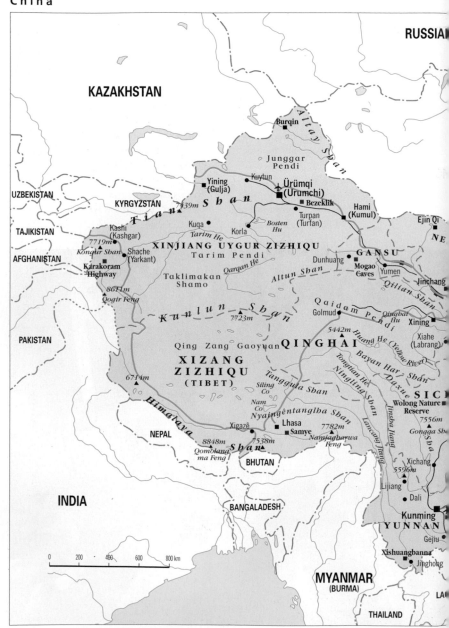

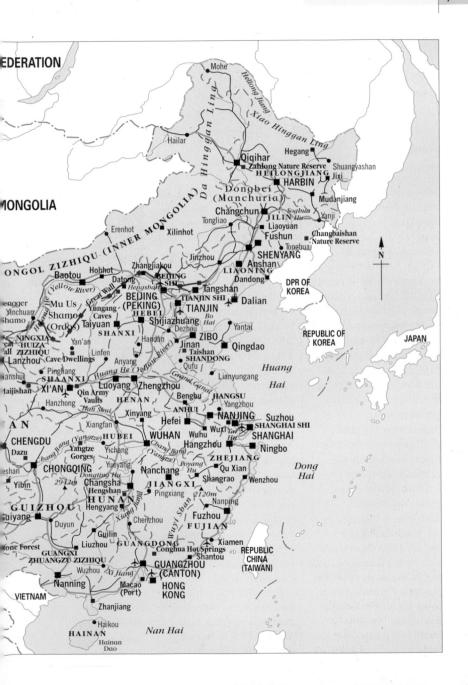

# The Land

China's landscape is written in superlatives. It has the second largest continuous stretch of land in the world (after Canada), and contains some of the planet's most notable landmarks, as well as the largest national population.

With a land area of some 9,600,000sq km (including Tibet), the People's Republic of China (Zhonghua Renmin Gonghe Guo in Chinese, or simply the PRC) counts a population of 1.3 billion people. Chinese territorial claims are disputed in Tibet. The PRC considers Taiwan to be an integral part of China, as indeed do the Taiwanese, except that they also consider their government to be the legitimate government of all China. Hong Kong and Macao are now Special Administrative Regions.

China, whose name means the Middle Kingdom, is bounded to the north by mountains and the Gobi Desert, to the west by the Himalayas, and to the east by an 18,000km coastline extending south along the Yellow Sea, the East China Sea and the South China Sea. The highest point is 8,848m, at the peak of Mount Everest in Tibet, and the lowest point is the Turpan (or Turfan) Depression of Xinjiang in the northwest, 154m below sea level.

## Borderline Cases

China has extensive borders, some disputed with neighbouring nations, Russia, Mongolia, North Korea, Vietnam, Laos, Myanmar (Burma), India, Bhutan, Nepal, Pakistan, Afghanistan, Kazakhstan, Kyrgyzstan, and Tajikistan. About 94 per cent of the population is Han Chinese (this includes 10 million or so related Muslim people called the Hui). The remainder is divided between 54 recognised minority nationalities (*see pp20–21*), some of Caucasian stock.

More than two-thirds of the country is composed of mountain, upland, high plateaux, desert and semi-desert. Some 90 per cent of

## THOMAS COOK'S CHINA

'The isolation of the vast Chinese Empire . . . will soon be a thing of the past. An agency now at work there – Cook's Tours – will do more to expedite the enlightening process and make the 'Open Door' an accomplished fact than any event since Marco Polo visited the land hundreds of years ago and told an unbelieving world of the wonders of China.'

From Cook's *American Traveller's Gazette*, December 1907.

the population lives in the coastal areas and flood-plains of great rivers such as a Yangtze (Chiang Jiang), the Yellow (Huang He), and the Pearl (Zhu Jiang) – zones under heavy ecological stress as a result of years of intensive farming and pollution.

## Climate
It is difficult to generalise about China's climate. There are seven recognised zones: the northeast, noted for humid summers and bitterly cold winters; central China, whose coastal regions are prone to tropical cyclones; tropical and subtropical south China; the southwest, where mountains moderate the summer temperatures; the high, mountain-fringed plateau of Tibet; the arid deserts of Xinjiang; and the extreme seasonal variability of Inner Mongolia.

From a visitor's point of view, a compromise is necessary, because China experiences climatic extremes at almost all times of the year. Temperatures can range from minus 40°C during winter in Inner Mongolia, to plus 40°C during the hot southern summer. Spring and autumn are liable to be the best times to travel, and facilities will not be swamped by the summer rush. Of course, this can vary locally depending on festivals.

The country is divided into 22 provinces (Anhui, Fujian, Gansu, Guangdong, Guizhou, Hainan, Hebei, Heilongjiang, Henan, Hubei, Hunan, Jiangsu, Jiangxi, Jilin, Liaoning, Qinghai, Shaanxi, Shandong, Shanxi, Sichuan, Yunnan and Zhejiang); three municipalities (Beijing, Shanghai and Tianjin); and five autonomous regions (Guangxi Zhuang, Nei Menggu (or Inner Mongolia), Ningxia Hui, Xinjiang Uygar, and Xizang (or Tibet).

Every inch of fertile land is used for growing commercial crops

# History

Chinese history moves to its own majestic rhythm. Dynasties come and go on the Dragon Throne, some leaving only a brief legacy of brutal unification, others basking in the warm afterglow of a golden age. Periods of chaos and civil war mark the interregnums. Grand ideas – Confucianism, Taoism, Buddhism – clash along the corridors of time. The modern era witnesses the same great game: only the players and ideologies have changed. Communism awaits history's verdict as China stands on the cusp of a new economic and political era.

Ancient Chinese bronze sculpture

Like traces of faded ink on an ancient ricepaper document, the first indicators of a Chinese civilisation emerged from the mists of Stone Age prehistory. The Yangshao and Longshan cultures, which gave rise to the shadowy Xia dynasty, the first in China's long progression of dynasties, left behind them a record in the form of finely made and beautifully decorated pottery.

A farming and metal-working culture grew up around 1500 BC along the flood-plain of the Yellow River in northern China, and in the surrounding hills. The people of this Shang kingdom valued jade and made tripod cauldrons of bronze, decorated with sacred symbols, for rituals in honour of their gods and ancestors. This was China's heroic age, a time of warriors, chariots, royal hunts, and human sacrifice.

Soon after 1100 BC, the Shang were overrun by the warlike Zhou. In time, these new masters of the 'Middle Kingdom' were assimilated into the Shang's agricultural theocracy. The Zhou kingdom gradually split into a mosaic of mutually antagonistic city-states, and the king became a figure-head ruling from the sacred capital, Luoyang. This is reflected in the chronological division of the era into a Western Zhou (1066–771 BC) and an Eastern Zhou (770–475 BC) period, with the latter dissolving into the Warring States period (475–221 BC).

Throughout the Zhou era, the kingdom was extended south towards the Yangtze River. By its end, cast iron had begun to replace bronze for weaponry and tools, and the ox-drawn plough was taking over from human traction in the fields. It was a time of ferment in political, social and moral issues, when rulers valued sages for their advice on correct behaviour and enlightened political rule. Confucius was the greatest of these philosophers.

## The Great Wall Rises
In 221 BC, the northwestern state of Qin won the war between the states. The Qin

dynasty did not rule for long, but its first emperor, the brilliant but brutal Qin Shihuang, unified China and began the construction of the Changcheng (Great Wall), which would eventually stretch for 6,500km, to defend his kingdom against the northern barbarians. He also standardised weights, measures, and writing, and unified thought by burning all books except those on medicine, agriculture, and divination. Scholars with contrary opinions were wise to keep their heads down – Qin Shihuang had his opponents buried alive. His successor was overthrown in 206 BC by Liu Bang, who founded the Han dynasty, ushering in a golden age, with Confucianism as the state religion. Under the Emperor Wudi, China made contact with India,

and Buddhism seeped into Chinese culture. The Han also established control of the Silk Road, the main trade route across Asia to Europe. Paper and the water clock were invented, while astronomers learned to predict eclipses.

The Han dynasty collapsed in AD 220, following the revolt of the 'Yellow Turban' Taoist cult. With the breakdown of central authority, northern nomads penetrated the Great Wall.

The Three Kingdoms period followed, during which the states of Wei, Shu and Wu competed for dominance. Some of the drama of those turbulent times survives today in folklore, historical novels, and cinema. In 581, the Sui re-established central control and ruled brutally for a short time, before giving way to a new dynasty.

Terracotta warriors, Shaanxi History Museum, Xi'an

## The Tang Renaissance

Comparable in its impact with the European Renaissance, the Tang dynasty, which ruled from 618 to 907, made giant strides forward in literacy, art, science and economic growth. Establishing their capital at Changan (present-day Xi'an), the Tang emperors created a vast bureaucracy.

Construction of the Grand Canal was begun. Chinese porcelain acquired a reputation for excellence which it has never lost. Gunpowder was invented, woodblock printing began, and presses were established. The second Tang emperor, Taizong, was followed by a remarkable woman, the Empress Wu, who poisoned her way to power and ruled from 660 until 705.

When the last Tang emperor, Li Tzu, abdicated in 907, division and civil war followed in the period of the Five Dynasties and Ten Kingdoms. Zhao Kuangyin established the Song Dynasty in 960, broke the power of rival warlords, and restored central administration, with the capital at Kaifeng. It was later transferred to Hangzhou, dividing the Song Dynasty into a Northern and a Southern Song period. Painting was elevated to its highest level, and a revolution of ideas brought about a reappraisal of the tenets of Confucianism and Buddhism.

## The Mongol Invasion

The spectre of invasion, hanging permanently over the north, became a reality when the Mongol leader, Kublai Khan, the grandson of Genghiz Khan, swept away the Song Dynasty in 1279. So began the Mongol-led Yuan dynasty. With its capital at Beijing, and its pleasure gardens at Hangzhou and Suzhou, it raised graceful living to an art form that astonished the Italian explorer, Marco Polo. Kublai Khan's successors saw Mongol power fade through constant rebellions, and a natural disaster when the Yellow River changed its course, flooding a vast territory.

The reins of power were snatched up by the Ming emperors in 1368, and for nearly three centuries the Ming dynasty unified China: Beijing's Forbidden City was built during their time. A peasant revolt

## THE CULTURAL REVOLUTION

Unleashed in 1967, this was Mao Zedong's vehicle for freeing the Party, society and culture of the old values that were preventing the attainment of 'pure' Communism. He issued a call to the Red Guards to reignite the original fire of the revolution. For 10 years, China was at the whim of the ageing Mao's prejudices and fantasies, until the purging threatened to shatter the country entirely. Much of inestimable value in art, architecture, science and literature was destroyed, and a terrible price was paid in terms of lives lost, and others permanently broken by torture and banishment.

brought down the Ming after decades of famine, but the peasant leaders had not secured full control before a Manchu army invaded, capturing Beijing in 1644. The Manchu Qing emperors extended their rule deep into Central Asia and to the Himalayas. In the early 19th century Western colonial powers began a series of incursions into China.

The last emperor was replaced in 1911 by a republic, an unstable foundation that had to deal with Communist insurgency and Japanese invasion. Civil war between Communists and Nationalists followed the end of World War II, with the victorious Communists, led by Mao Zedong, establishing the People's Republic in 1949; the Nationalists, under Chiang Kaishek, retreated to Taiwan.

Mao's death in 1976 opened the door for a curious hybrid form of Communism, led by his successor Deng Xiaoping, employing market economics, but with the Communist Party firmly in control – as democracy supporters in Tiananmen Square found to their cost in 1989. By the time of his death in 1997, Deng had laid the foundation for solid economic growth unprecedented in Chinese history.

The conflict between democratic forces and the Communist Party has continued into the 21st century, though Hong Kong's return to Chinese rule presents new challenges. If China manages to rule and sustain this vibrant economic entity with fairness, it may not be long before Taiwan seeks to rejoin the mainland.

Ceramic jars in the Banpo museum, Xi'an, Shaanxi

# The Long March

Mao Zedong (1893–1976) led the Communist revolution in China that, in 1949, added one-fifth of the human race to the roster of nations grouped under the red banner. Few individuals match so perfectly with their time and place that they have such a major impact on the world. Chairman Mao, the first red emperor of China, born into a farming family in Hunan province, was one such.

Today, Mao's portrait is no longer ubiquitous, and his 'little Red Book', The Thoughts of Chairman Mao, is a long way down the bestseller lists, but Mao still commands respect from ordinary Chinese. This is evident in the way the crowds shuffle respectfully past his embalmed body at his mausoleum in Beijing. After graduating from a teachers' training college in Changsha, Mao moved to Beijing where, in 1921, he became a founding member of the Chinese Communist Party. In 1923, the Communists forged an alliance with the Nationalists, and together the 'united front' consolidated power in southern and central China. In 1926, however, the alliance ended in armed conflict and the Communists were driven out of their strongholds. Mao learned two lessons from this: that guerrilla tactics were the way forward, and that 'political power grows through the barrel of a gun'.

Mao settled in Jiangxi province, but the Nationalists were determined to destroy their former allies. In October 1934, Nationalist forces drove Mao and his followers from the province, and thus began the Long March. Trekking more than 9,500km across China, with some 86,000 men, Mao intended to find a new and more secure base in Shaanxi province from which to pursue his 'people's war'. The epic march, across some of the roughest country on the earth, took a year, and only 6,000 of his troops survived. Yet it was from his secure foothold in Shaanxi that Mao would emerge to take over China 15 years later.

Mao's leadership of the Long March made him a figure of legend and authority

# Governance

China's stability and growing prosperity has been dearly bought as, over the years, the Communists have fought to impose their doctrine, and the ruling caste has sought to maintain its power. The most recent example of this was the massacre, by the People's Liberation Army, of over 2,000 young pro-democracy protesters in Beijing's Tiananmen Square in 1989.

The Chinese flag

The People's Republic of China was proclaimed in 1949 after the Communist forces of Mao Zedong won a hard-fought war against the Nationalist Kuomintang government of Chiang Kaishek. In 1950, Chiang fled to Taiwan (then known as Formosa). China became – or, more accurately, continued to be – a one-party state, this time with the Chinese Communist Party in the driving seat.

Under the government's first five-year plan, great stress was placed on nationalisation, the development of heavy industry, and collectivisation of agriculture, the intention being to drag China from the feudal age into the modern world. The Great Leap Forward, initiated in 1958, emphasised the development of local political structures under Communist Party control, and the establishment of rural communes. It also led to the death of millions in the famine that followed.

**Purists versus Pragmatists**
Intellectuals began to chafe under the restrictions placed on their freedom of expression. In partial response to this,

the party launched its Hundred Flowers movement under the slogan: 'Let a Hundred Flowers Bloom and a Hundred Schools of Thought Contend'. Those who took advantage of the apparent openness to voice anti-government opinions were identified and purged.

The struggle continued between those who supported Mao in preaching revolutionary fervour, and the pragmatists who were willing to ditch much Communist baggage in favour of progress – with the crucial exception that the party had absolutely no intention of relaxing its monopoly on political power.

As Mao and his supporters felt their control of the party slipping away to what they considered 'capitalist roaders', Mao struck back with the Great Proletarian Cultural Revolution in 1967. For 10 years, China remained in the grip of an ailing Mao's obsession with permanent revolution. Youthful Red Guards launched a wave of terror in which opponents were banished to the countryside, tortured, or killed.

Mao's death in 1976 and the arrest of his closest supporters (the so-called

Gang of Four, including Mao's wife, Jiang Qing) cleared the way for the next party chairman, Deng Xiaoping.

## Pragmatism Rules

Deng introduced more pragmatic policies in the economic sphere, flirting openly with capitalism and releasing the native energy and business skills of the Chinese, allowing them to benefit personally while developing the country's overall economy. With the death of Deng even more freedom appears to have been given. Recent years have even seen a small-scale introduction of a voting system in some areas to elect village leaders and communities, pointing the way towards a kind of democracy. Indeed, President Jiang Zemin and premier Zhu Rongji have done their utmost to promote international trade to make sure the open-door policy never slams shut – China's hosting of world summits such as Fortune 500 and APEC (Asia Pacific Economic Cooperation) are major examples – China is today a member of the World Trade Organization; and Hong Kong and Macao's return to

China have heralded a new tolerance to Western-style government. However, despite many changes, freedom of speech is still very much taboo, an example being the suppression of Fa Long Gong supporters, but there is a great deal of hope among the youth of China for their motherland, the 'sleeping dragon'.

Above: traffic police try hard to control the frenzy on the roads; Below: Palace Museum, Tiananmen Gate with giant portrait of Chairman Mao at the entrance

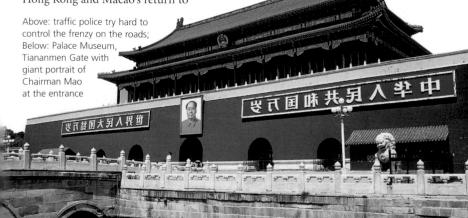

# Culture

Defining the culture of 1.3 billion people is no easy task, although it is somewhat simplified by the fact that 94 per cent of them are Han Chinese, sharing a common history that dates back at least 5,000 years.

The Chinese are proud of their culture and its continuity, even if they do occasionally look to the outside world for models of progress. That cultural pride, the sense of being part of something greater than the individual, a social structure that has stood the test of time, is part of the innate feeling of superiority most Chinese feel towards those unlucky enough not to have been born Chinese.

This does not mean the 'average' Chinese is always culturally aware. In a real sense they care less about the great talismans of their culture – Confucianism, imperial dynasties, painting, calligraphy – than many tourists. Partly this is because the effort of daily living can be hard enough. Even religion, among the few who still practise it, has a profoundly practical aspect, whereby the gods are expected to reward their supplicants with health, wealth or advancement.

## Artistic Heritage

Collectively known as the 'four treasures of the

## FACE, AND HOW NOT TO LOSE IT

Face is important in China. It shows itself in subtle ways, particularly with foreign visitors. The madder a foreigner gets at the lack of reaction (inscrutability, if you will) of a Chinese who doesn't seem to be getting the message, the smaller he becomes in the eye of the beholder. This can make travelling in China hard on the nerves, because the country throws up heaps of situations which seem to call for vociferous complaint. The Chinese are not averse to shouting among themselves, but foreigners should be patient and under-standing at all times.

Peking Opera performance (above), and a game of draughts (facing page), both of ancient pedigree

studio', the brush, paper, ink stick and ink stone are the basic 'ingredients' of Chinese painting and calligraphy. In every painting, it is said, there is a poem, and in every poem a painting, and so the arts of painting and calligraphy are linked in spirit. Music is richly ornamented and often employs abstract and atonal patterns; it, too, has a very ancient pedigree. Among its instruments are the *qin* (a kind of zither), the *dizi* (a bamboo flute), and the *pipa* (a pear-shaped lute). Music is popular with the ordinary people. There are also other highly stylised forms developed for the imperial court, and for Chinese opera.

It is very difficult, looking at the graceless modern tower blocks that are mushrooming in China's cities, to remember that traditional Chinese buildings represent one of the world's distinctive architectural forms. This is so because, apart from pagodas, most buildings, including temples and palaces, were made of wood, which meant that they frequently burned down. Most surviving ancient buildings (such as Beijing's Forbidden City) date from the Ming dynasty, and are noted for their complex symmetrical plans, colourful pavilions, and curved roofs.

## Troubled Times

Chinese culture is still recovering from the shock the Cultural Revolution unleashed by Mao Zedong between 1967 and 1976. Temples, books, paintings, poetry, and opera – all were consumed by the fires of zealotry spread by the Red Guards. Mao's attempt to draw a line between the old society and the new by erasing the collective memory of the past failed, partly through sheer exhaustion.

Even so, the Chinese themselves are still discovering what their culture is, even as they live it out every day; most are busy taking advantage of the new freedom to get ahead fast while they can, even as they remain aware that in the long sweep of Chinese history, good times have often given way to bad.

## Tribal China

The distinction between tribal and
'ordinary' minorities became blurred
after the 1949 Communist takeover. The
collectivisation of agriculture was also
applied to tribal groups. The
Mongolians are perhaps the best-known
tribal minority, at least in the sense that
many foreigners have a vague notion of
where Mongolians live – in Inner
Mongolia, where they are a one in five
minority, even in their own homeland.
Many of their half million or so people
have clung on to their nomadic
traditions, living in a portable hide tent
called a *gher* (similar to a *yurt*).

Some 2.5 million Manchus, heirs to a
warrior tradition, survive with a distinct
identity in the northeast, although their
horse-borne days are now over. Other
groups, like the Oroqen, have been
persuaded, not least by the comforts and

China's minority peoples often retain their
distinctive style of dress

A family from Xiahe, northwest China

conveniences of modern society, to adopt a more settled lifestyle. The Han Chinese allow the tribes some cultural autonomy but retain effective political and economic power in their own hands. *(See also* Minorities, *p92.)*

China's invasion of Tibet (*see p136*) in 1950–51 was followed by repression and the flight of the Dalai Lama, god-ruler of the country's Buddhist people. Tibetan religious treasures were devastated during the Cultural Revolution, and China continues to occupy Tibet, with Han immigrants to ensure Beijing's continuing control over the territory.

Members of the Dai ethnic community from the Kunming region

# Confucianism, Taoism, and Buddhism

## Confucianism

The stereotypical 'Chinaman' of Hollywood films was always ready with some anodyne saying from Confucius, reflecting the fact that Confucian thought still permeates Chinese society, as it has done for 2,500 years. Many educated Chinese can quote knowledgeably from the great philosopher, whose real name was Kong Fuzi (Kung Fu-tse), the Master Kong. Born in the 6th century BC, at Qufu, in the state of Lu (present-day Shandong province), Confucius spent most of his life as a government official.

The *Confucian Analects*, compiled after his death, are a collection of his sayings and actions, which are themselves based on ancient Chinese teachings and precepts. The origins of nature, believed Confucius, are to be found in the yin-yang, passive-active principles, which form a harmony when combined. In practice, he stressed social justice, filial piety, and the obligations of the ruler towards the ruled and vice versa. The religious element in his teaching was based on the notion that if individuals and society behaved properly, heaven would leave them in peace.

## Taoism

Taoism is based on the teachings of Lao Zi, the Old Master, a 6th-century BC philosopher. Nothing is known about the life of Lao Zi (who may, in fact, be legendary). His teachings, compiled in the 3rd century BC, were at least partly in opposition to those of Confucius. In the *Dao De Jing* the Tao, or Way, is the hidden principle at the heart of the universe, a principle which can be touched by those prepared to live in harmony with nature and the environment. This was in contrast to the focus on right behaviour and good deeds advocated by Confucius.

As Taoism developed, its belief system also incorporated the yin-yang (female-male) system of balancing opposites.

## Buddhism

Buddhism was imported from India. *Karma* is Buddhism's main doctrine: the belief that good and evil deeds beget their own reward, both in this life, but more so in the future, through reincarnation. By the time of its widespread acceptance in China, Buddhism had undergone significant changes. The concept of Paradise became a key part of Chinese Buddhism in the

Mahayana form of Buddhism, called Chan in China, a variation of which took root in Japan as Zen. The idea that a Buddhist monk should be able to look after himself led to the foundation of the Shaolin Monastery near Dengfeng, in Henan province, where the Kung Fu form of self-defence combat was developed. However, more Chinese still admit to practising Taoism than Buddhism.

**Modern Beliefs**

Today, although the government has softened its stance since the days of the Cultural Revolution and some Confucian temples have even been restored, religion is still a sensitive subject. The state's on-going repression of Fa Long Gong, an alternate method of self

healing and mind control, is well known, and many still look upon traditional beliefs with scepticism. Older people continue to go on pilgrimages to temples or holy mountains, but the younger generation today regard these as tourist attractions, and have scant regard for the peace and aura of such a place.

Facing page: statue of Confucius
Above: Buddhist (left) and Taoist (right) monks
Below: joss sticks and paper offerings

# Festivals

Festivals form an important part of China's respect for the past, although not all are public holidays. This is a selection of the more important national and local festivals, many of which are also celebrated in Hong Kong and Macao.

Incense sticks are always in great demand

### Harbin Ice and Snow Festival
*5 January–5 February*
The people of Heilongjiang province create fabulous, lit-up ice sculptures.

### Lantern Festival
*Mid-February–mid-March*
Home-made lanterns are displayed on the 15th day of the first moon.

### Tomb Sweep Day
*5 April*
Honouring ancestors by cleaning their tombs and placing flowers on them.

### Dai Nationality Water Sprinkling Festival
*13–15 April*
In the Kunming area, people of the Dai ethnic group celebrate life by splashing water on each other – the more water, the luckier and healthier one will be.

### Luoyang Peony Fair
*15–25 April*
The peony is celebrated against the backdrop of Luoyang's giant Buddha rock sculptures. More than a million blooms are on display in city parks.

### Weifang International Kite Festival
*20–25 April*
Home of the International Kite Federation and a Kite Museum, Weifang (in Shandong province) displays its love affair with kites.

### Hong Kong Dragon Boat Festival
*5th–7th day of the lunar month of May*
One of China's most famous festivals, honouring the water-borne version of the country's emblematic dragon.

### Yunnan Torch Festival
*23–25 July*
Minority nationalities hold a wide-ranging cultural festival, culminating in a torchlight procession in the Stone Forest near Kunming.

### Sichuan Torch Festival
*23–28 July*
Torchlight parades and other cultural performances of minority nationalities throughout Sichuan province.

### Nadam Fair and Grassland Tourism Festival
*15–25 August*
Held at Hohhot, capital of Inner Mongolia, this features folklore and traditional products, and also a flower fair and tour of Wudang Lamasery.

### Xuedun Festival
*Variable dates, usually in August*

The Tibetan yoghurt-banquet festival, held in Lhasa, includes performances of traditional Tibetan opera and dance.

## Xinjiang Grape Festival
*20–26 August*
The Yuelu Caravan of Camels is the highlight of this festival in Turpan, that recalls life along the ancient Silk Route.

## Xi'an Ancient Culture and Art Festival
*9–15 September*
Pageants recall the ancient cultures of this former capital of China, close to the site of the terracotta warriors.

## Shaolin Martial Arts Festival
*10–15 September*
The monks of Mount Songshan (Henan province) display their martial-arts skills.

## Suzhou International Silk Festival
*20–25 September*
During this silk fashion show, the city's imperial gardens are illuminated and used for garden parties.

## Chengdu International Panda Festival
*24–28 September*
Symposium on panda conservation, and visits to nearby Wolong Nature Reserve.

## Birthday of Confucius
*28 September*
Celebrates the great Chinese sage (*see p22*) throughout China, especially in his home town of Qufu (Shandong province).

## West Lake International Tour Boat Festival
*5–7 October*
On the old imperial lake at Hangzhou, a feast of traditional costumes and gaily decorated tour boats.

## Three Gorges Art Festival
*20–25 October (every second year)*
A celebration in Yichang (Hubei province) of the arts and crafts of the Yangtze River's Three Gorges area, soon to be submerged by the Yangtze River dam project (*see p58*).

Hong Kong's celebrated Dragon Boat Festival is a test of skill and stamina

# Impressions

Possessed of a well-nigh inexhaustible supply of people, customs and languages, China is a hard country to come to grips with, and harder still to understand. There are no easy alternatives to climbing down from the silver palanquin of an organised tour and joining the Chinese in the ways of everyday life. The going may be hard, but the reward is an insight into one of the world's most fascinating societies as it struggles to reinvent itself.

Old people are the torch-bearers of tradition

There are times when the exasperated traveller in China might be forgiven for thinking it would be a wonderful country were it not for the Chinese. Not that, as individuals, they are any better or worse per se than the people of any other nationality, but they are more often encountered in groups, and in groups their behaviour can be hard to bear. If you have just been trampled in the rush to get on a train with no reserved seats, or been caught in the line of fire of someone spitting out of the window of a bus, it may be hard to maintain a Confucian self-detachment. Still, it is their country, and part of the joy of travel is the chance to experience different patterns of life, and the Chinese are certainly different.

## Overcrowding

One of the most obvious truths about the Chinese is that there are a great many of them. The impact of the vast population, mainly crowded into the fertile one-fifth of their land, is apparent at all times, particularly in city streets or on swamped public transport systems.

Thoughtful Chinese themselves draw attention to this fact, saying gloomily that there are 'too many people', though whether it is overcrowded apartments that depress them most, or the spectre of ultimate starvation, they do not say. (This last point is no joke: the Washington-based Earthwatch Institute predicts a shortfall of some 216 million tonnes of grain per year in China by the year 2030, against total world exports to all grain-importing countries that have never gone above 200 million tonnes.)

## Great Expectorations

Spitting may be the great social disease in China – literally, since the phlegm deposited so liberally helps retain the pool of viruses from which various brands of 'Chinese flu' arise. The familiar sound of someone clearing the farthermost recesses of their lungs is a warning to be ready to spring out of the way. Almost everyone spits: young and old, male and female, simple folk and educated, both indoors and out. The government occasionally launches 'no-spitting' drives, but with little success.

Few other personal habits could be as annoying as this one, but then, some tourists' personal habits may be every bit as nauseating to their Chinese hosts.

Efforts are still made to limit the contact between foreigners and ordinary people, though this is far less prevalent than it was in the past, and few Chinese, certainly in the more cosmopolitan areas, would now be concerned about the political risks of speaking to foreigners. Yet in hotels and restaurants, and often on boats and trains, such segregation does exist. A more disagreeable practice is to charge foreigners up to 50 times the amount

禁止吸烟
NO SMOKING
请勿随地吐痰
DO NOT SPIT EVERYWHERE

Despite government campaigns, even China's leaders smoke heavily and spitting is endemic

that the Chinese pay for everything from train tickets to museum entries.

The bicycle is still the most popular means of transport – Bicycle parking, Beijing

## Essence of China

Landscape and climate are determinants of culture, quite as much as a shared heritage of ideas and art. In this respect, Chinese culture bridges the vast distance between the tropical forests of the southwest, the frozen plains of Manchuria and Inner Mongolia, the roof of the world in the Himalaya, the flood plains of the mighty Yangtze and Yellow Rivers, and the economically burgeoning coastal zone. Language changes over the vast distances involved, as do styles of architecture, cuisine, and even dress.

The idea of China, the essence of Chineseness, is nevertheless rooted deeply in the very bones of the people. They may see all kinds of differences among themselves, and be envious of the prosperity and freedom enjoyed by the advanced Western nations, but they have no doubt that to be Chinese is best.

The one-child-per-family rule means that children are greatly indulged

## Imperial Offspring

Extended families provide a fallback security in hard times. The Chinese look after their senior citizens better (relative to available resources), and accord them more respect than is the case in many Western countries.

Children are a delight to all, especially because the 'one-child' policy means there are few opportunities to be so delighted – and despite the fact that single children are often so spoiled that they are known as 'little emperors'.

These children are growing up in a China that has already set its sights on acquiring material things. The smartly dressed crowds strolling along the Bund (embankment) in Shanghai, for example, are the target of envious stares (nothing more serious) from peasants straight off the train from the countryside. Those peasants, too, are trying to get in on the prosperity act: unofficial Western estimates say that as many as 150 million migrant workers are on the move in China.

## Language

China's principal language is Mandarin, a term that originates from the Portuguese word *mandar* (which means 'to govern'), used in connection with imperial officials who spoke their own 'official language'. Mandarin is now the native language of some three-quarters of the Chinese people, mostly in the centre and the north. The Beijing variant of Mandarin (minus the capital's characteristic 'burr') is the official language of the country and is called *putonghua* (meaning 'the common tongue').

Street vendors sell a range of newspapers and cheap publications

Cantonese, spoken mostly in the Guangdong province, and in Hong Kong and Macao, is the second language, and although the characters used in written Chinese are the same throughout China, the difference in the spoken version is comparable to that between English and German. Other important languages are Xiang and Gan in Hunan and Jiangxi provinces, Wu around Shanghai, Min in Fujian, and Hakka in the south. There are also dozens of dialect groups.

### Character Building

Few Chinese speak any foreign language, although learning English, Spanish, French and German is now in vogue, particularly among the young. Few foreign visitors speak any Chinese, so mutual incomprehension is the usual state of affairs. It is, however, easier than it might seem to learn the handful of words, phrases and numbers that can make one's contact with the Chinese both polite and a little more fruitful. In this respect, a little knowledge can go a long way.

As a character-based language, the spoken and written forms of Chinese are separate. From the visitor's point of view, the characters are likely to be meaningless anyway, although it is possible to learn the meaning of a few dozen of the most important. The *pinyin* system of romanising Chinese can be both helpful and confusing, but is fairly widely used. It can be useful to know the *pinyin* name for a destination you may be trying to find: for example, you are likely to find your way better if you ask not for the Great Hall of the People, but the Renmin Dahui Tang.

## GETTING AROUND

Of the four possible modes of travelling around China – bus, train, plane or boat – only the boat can be considered relaxing, and even here a few provisos must be added. However, it is important to remember that China has come a long way in a short time, and further improvements in its transport network are an integral part of government plans for the country's continued economic expansion.

Undercapacity, outdated equipment, inadequate investment, and staff who are often poorly motivated would be enough to dislocate any transportation system. In China, this is compounded by the great distances to be covered, and the forbidding nature of much of the terrain. In addition, growing prosperity has given the Chinese the desire to see the natural and man-made wonders of their own country. Coping with demand from the vast potential pool of travellers is not a task to be underestimated.

Foreigners on organised tours should have few complaints about transport, although some tours and visits are liable to cancellation at short (or zero) notice for reasons which are not always explained. Independent travellers have to accept things as they are and make the best of them. The best can be very good; the worst can be very bad.

### By Bus for Those with Strong Nerves

This form of transport is easily dealt with, if only because there are so few long-distance bus services that it is probably best not even to consider this as a means of travel. The extent and

Public transport is very cheap but is also overcrowded

condition of roads make this a wise decision, although in remote regions, where railways do not reach, there is no alternative. Intercity and regional bus services are better, but far from luxurious. Only people with strong nerves should sit near the driver, with a clear view of how he handles the 'threat' of oncoming traffic: the near-suicidal disregard of danger will surely leave most observers shaken.

### By Train – China's Lifeline

Railways are China's arteries, the only more or less reliable way of getting from A to B. Without them the country would suffer some kind of fatal seizure. Trying to even get on a train might do the same for foreign travellers. It is important to have sharp elbows, a note in Chinese stating the ticket type desired, and a willingness to kowtow to the ticket clerk, who will pronounce with the finality of an emperor on one's travel plans.

If you find the right platform in an overcrowded station, the rest should go smoothly. Riding soft class, or soft class sleeper, is a good way to travel in China; you are provided with bunks, mostly clean linen, curtains, and meals in a dining car. Hard class is something else – particularly a hard seat on a long-distance train, though a hard sleeper can also be grim. Virtually the entire country is connected to the rail network. This is the way most Chinese travel.

On the two-day journey from Guangzhou (Canton) to Shanghai, the train crosses the heartland of China, taking in rivers, mountains, villages and cities, while the aggravations of a developing country's booming economy are soothed away to the beat of steel-shod wheels on rails. A postcard-in-motion unfolds through the windows – a panoply of fields worked by peasants wearing conical hats. The work in those fields is hard, you tell yourself as you pass through, but it seems a timeless image of pastoral peace. Only a master of Chinese painting could capture the landscape's many moods.

Such experiences are the stuff of train travel in China, and if there are others which are less desirable – overcrowded stations, dirty trains, unhelpful staff – together they create a unique vantage point for observing China. The country loves its railways, warts and all, and could scarcely survive without them. Most provincial capitals are already connected to Beijing and the others

Steam still rules the rails in several parts of China

soon will be. The steam engines, which once captured romantic imaginations, are giving way to diesel units, and many lines are being electrified. Air-conditioning has even put in an appearance on prestige routes. On China's railways, the times, and timetables, are changing, but the experience is still unforgettable.

### Jet Setters

Forget the days of deck-chairs in the gangway to accommodate extra passengers, and pilots who thought they were flying the Chinese version of the MiG-19 jet fighter. Civil aviation in China is growing up, assisted by joint ventures with international carriers (Dragonair's link with Cathay Pacific, for example). A fleet of new airliners is now in service, so you can expect to fly in reliable aeroplanes, like the Boeing 737, McDonnell Douglas MD11, Airbus A320, and British Aerospace 146.

A report in *Business Week* called China a 'leading contender for the title of the most dangerous place in the world to fly', with aircraft not always perfectly maintained, and pilots averaging 280 flight hours a month (rules set a limit of 100). Higher standards are now being implemented – passengers can no longer get out of their seats during take-off and landing!

## THOMAS COOK'S CHINA

'The first real railway line in China was opened last September with unexpected éclat, between Tientsin [Tianjin], Taku and Tongshan. The length of the line is only eighty-six and a half miles [138km], but the success achieved is a great factor towards future development in this direction . . .'
From Cook's *Excursionist and Tourist Advertiser*, 14 December 1888.

River ferries travel huge distances

## Ferrying Across

While the train is the most flexible way to travel long distances, few experiences beat travelling by boat. Most such trips are likely to be in the form of an organised excursion, but independent travellers can hop aboard services such as the Yangtze River cruise boats plying between Chongqing to Wuhan or Shanghai. The jetcat on the Pearl River is an ideal way to get between Hong Kong and Guangzhou (Canton). Macao is connected to Canton by ferry. Other possibilities include excursions on the Grand Canal (between Hangzhou and Suzhou), on the Li River (from Guilin), the Yellow River, and on various lakes.

## Other Modes

Taxis are fast and easy to hire, though honest taxi drivers seem to be rationed to one per province. Buses and minibuses are not bad once routes and timetables have been figured out, but are almost always packed. Pedicabs and scooter-cabs are fine, but many drivers have a flexible interpretation of what constitutes a fair agreement.

In Beijing, the subway is a good alternative to the bus, although it can be hot and stuffy. Finally, the humble bicycle may be the perfect way to get around, particularly as walking may be difficult because of the long distances involved.

China's railways sweep across the country in all directions

# The Main Sights

A terracotta warrior from Xi'an

China is big and few people have the opportunity to return time after time, so your aim will probably be to see as many of the main attractions as possible on your visit. This will also be the aim, unfortunately, of just about all your fellow tourists, and that includes a fair percentage of the country's own population as well.

This means that the most popular places, such as the site of the terracotta warriors at Xi'an, may seem like madhouses. There is not much to be done about this, apart from avoiding such locations altogether, which would seem to defeat the purpose of going to China in the first place.

Beijing, with its Forbidden City, the Temple of Heaven, and the Summer Palace, is in the north, and the Great Wall is not far away. Further north are the vast spaces of Inner Mongolia, while in the far northeast is Harbin, famed for its winter ice sculptures. Shanghai, China's most vibrant and exciting city, as well as its most modern, is situated on the east coast. Relatively close to Shanghai (as far as Chinese distances go) are the beautiful and historic cities of Suzhou, Hangzhou, Wuxi, and Nanjing.

Xi'an, famous for its terracotta warriors, occupies a fairly isolated position in mountainous country in the northern central part of China, with Chengdu a lengthy hop over the mountains to the southwest. The two great rivers, the Yangtze (Chiang Jiang) and the Yellow (Huang He), draw muddy swathes across middle China, the former following a southerly track, and the latter a more northerly one. Guangzhou (Canton) faces Hong Kong and Macao on the southeastern coast, with Guilin's famous limestone hills to its northwest, and Kunming, gateway to the south, to its west.

Xinjiang Autonomous Region, an enormous mass of land which is, however, sparsely populated, fills in the western zone, and reaches toward the Himalaya and beyond.

Summer Palace, Beijing

Many maps in China can be bought fairly cheaply from street vendors

# Beijing

With a population of almost 11 million, Beijing is one of three special metropolitan areas in China (the others are Shanghai and Tianjin), separate from provincial control. As the national capital, Beijing is really in a special category of its own. While Shanghai and Guangzhou, among other cities, are far more vibrant economically, Beijing is the city of grace and style, lavishly endowed with the best of everything by the Communist Party top brass, if only because they have to live here too.

Beihai Park was once the private retreat of emperors

Add to this the rush towards economic growth that everywhere grips the country, and Beijing is fast developing as a world capital. The city has the ambitions that go along with such a status, and, increasingly, it has the resources to satisfy them, together with a legacy of unique historic monuments and an infrastructure that, although strained, is better able to cope with increasing demands than many other Chinese cities.

## Ancient Observatory (Guguan Xiangtai)

The tower was built in 1279 to house the astronomical observatory. It once held the bronze observational instruments from which Chinese astrologers got the data that they would present in horoscopes to the emperor.
*2 Dongbiaobei Hutong.*
*Tel: (010) 6524 2202/2246.*
*Off Jianguomen Wai Ave, near the Friendship Store.*
*Open: Wed–Sun 9–11am & 1–4.30pm.*
*Metro: Jianguomen station.*

## Beihai Park (Beihai Gongyuan)

There can be few more beautiful city parks in the world than this graceful former retreat of the emperors, situated slightly north and west of the Forbidden City. Located on the site of a 10th-century palace, many of its structures are reconstructions of originals dating from the 15th to the 17th centuries. Covering almost 70 hectares, half of which is taken up by Beihai Lake, the park is notable for the Round City, adjacent to the south gate, an area established by the Mongol Emperor Kublai Khan (1214–1294) for his palace. At the heart of Beihai Lake is the Jade Islet, whose monumental buildings include the Hall of Universal Peace, and the ghostly bubble of the **White Dagoba**.
*1 Wenjin Ave. Tel: (010) 6403 2244.*
*Open: daily 6am–8pm. Admission charge.*
*There are four gates: north, east, south, and west.*

## Beijing Zoo (Beijing Dongwuyuan)

Even the famed pandas don't have much

in the way of room or anything at all that even appears like a recreated natural habitat. None of this seems to bother the Chinese, who love the zoo, which is notable also for its tigers, yaks, and sea turtles, among many other species on display. *Xizhimen Wai St. Tel: (010) 6831 4411. Open: daily 7.30am–5.30pm (Panda Hall 8am–5pm). Admission charge. Nearest subway station is Xizhimen, then take any westbound trolley-bus.*

## China Art Gallery (Zhongguo Meishu Guan)

Formerly the Peking University building, opened to the public in 1959 and recently totally refurbished, the gallery features constantly changing exhibitions of Chinese arts and crafts. *1 Wusi St. Located east of Coal Hill. Tel: (010) 6401 6234. Open: Tue–Sun 9am–4pm. Closed: Mon. Admission charge.*

## Coal Hill, Jingshan Park (Jingshan Gongyuan)

Also known as Prospect Hill, this five-peaked artificial hill provided the emperors with a view over the city from within their private park (they also apparently maintained a supply of coal beneath it, hence its other name). Now open to the public, the park still has superb views, and splendid pavilions from which to appreciate them. *44 Jingshanxi Ave. Located just to the north of the Forbidden City. Tel: (010) 6404 4071. Open: daily 6am–9pm. Admission charge.*

The Empress Cixi's boat is moored at the Summer Palace, Beijing

# Beijing

Contemplation on Coal Hill

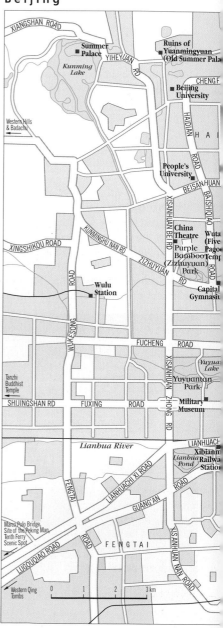

## Confucian Temple (Kong Miao)

Now operating as the Capital Museum, the temple was founded in 1302 but, like just about every historic structure in Beijing, it has been destroyed and restored innumerable times since then. It is a curiously antiseptic place, devoid of the natural activity you would associate with a temple. Its main interest lies in its inscribed stone steles, some of them said to be around 2,500 years old. *13 Guozijian St. Opposite the Lama Temple, off Yonghegong St. Tel: (010) 6407 3593. Open: Tue–Sun 9am–5pm. Closed: Mon. Admission charge.*

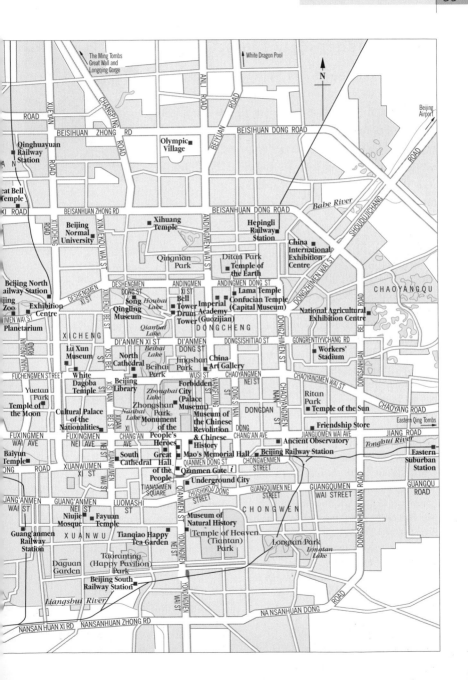

The Ming Tombs
Great Wall and
Longqing Gorge

White Dragon Pool

N

Beijing
Airport

ROAD

XUEYAN

CHANGPING ROAD

ANLI ROAD

BEIYUAN ROAD

BEISIHUAN DONG ROAD

BEISIHUAN ZHONG RD

Qinghuayuan
Railway
Station

Olympic
Village

SHOUDUJICHANG ROAD

eat Bell
emple

KI ROAD

BEISANHUAN ZHONG RD

XITUCHENG ROAD

XINJIEKOU WAI ST

Xihuang
Temple

ANDINGMEN WAI ST

BEISANHUAN DONG ROAD

Babe River

Beijing
Normal
University

Hepingli
Railway
Station

China
International
Exhibition
Centre

DONGZHIMEN WAI ST

CHAOYANGQU

Qingnian
Park

Ditan Park
Temple of
the Earth

Beijing North
ailway Station

ijing
Zoo    Exhibition
       Centre

IMEN WAI ST

Planetarium

DESHENGMEN
DONG ST

DESHENGMEN
XI ST

XINJIEKOU BEI ST

ANDINGMEN

Song  Houhai
Qingling Lake
Museum

Qianhai
Lake

ANDINGMEN DONG ST

Bell
XI ST
Tower
Imperial
Drum  Academy
Tower (Guozijian)

Lama Temple
Confucian Temple
(Capital Museum)

DONGZHIMEN ST

National Agricultural
Exhibition Centre

X I C H E N G

DONGCHENG

DI'ANMEN XI ST

Lu Xun
Museum

XISI BEI ST

Beihai
Lake

North
Cathedral

DI'ANMEN
DONG ST

DONGSISHITIAO ST

GONGRENTIYUCHANG RD

Workers'
Stadium

DONGSANHUAN

White
Dagoba
Temple

XISI NAN ST

Beijing
Library

Beihai
Park

Jingshan  China
Park      Art Gallery

WUSI ST

CHAOYANGMEN
NEI ST

CHAOYANGMEN WAI ST

Yuetan
Park

Temple of
the Moon

NANHAI ROAD

Cultural Palace
of the
Nationalities

XIDAN BEI ST

Zhongnan
Lake

Nanhai
Lake

Zhongshan
Park
Monument
of the
People's
Heroes

Forbidden
City
(Palace
Museum)

Museum of
the Chinese
Revolution
& Chinese
History

WANGFUJING

DONG SI NAN ST

DONGDAN

CHAOYANGMEN
NAN
ST

Ritan
Park
Temple of the Sun

Friendship Store

CHAOYANG ROAD

Eastern Qing Tombs

FUXINGMEN
WAI AVE

FUXINGMEN
NEI AVE

CHANG'AN
AVE

CHANG'AN AVE

DONG
CHANG'AN AVE

Ancient Observatory

JIANGUOMEN WAI AVE

JIANG ROAD

Tongbui River

Eastern
Suburban
Station

Baiyun
Temple

ONG    ROAD

XUANWUMEN
NEI AVE

South
Cathedral

XUANWUMEN
XI ST

Great
Hall
of the
People

Mao's Memorial Hall
QIANMEN DONG ST
Qianmen Gate i

Underground City

CHONGWENMEN
STREET

Beijing Railway Station

GUANGQU
ROAD

JANG'ANMEN
WAI ST

GUANG'ANMEN
NEI ST

LUOMASHI

TIANANMEN
SQUARE

QIANMEN ST

THUSHIKOU DONG
STREET

GUANGQUMEN NEI
STREET

GUANGQUMEN
WAI STREET

DONGSANHUAN NAN ROAD

Guang'anmen
Railway
Station

X U A N W U

Niujie  Fayuan
Mosque Temple

Tianqiao Happy
Tea Garden

YONGDINGMEN
NEI ST

Museum of
Natural History

C H O N G W E N

Temple of Heaven
(Tiantan)
Park

Longtan Park

Longtan
Lake

Daguan
Garden

Taoranting
(Happy Pavilion)
Park

Beijing South
Railway Station

YONGDINGMEN
WAI ST

Liangshui River

NA NSANHUAN DONG

ROAD

NANSAN HUAN XI RD   NANSANHUAN ZHONG RD

# The Forbidden City (Zijin Cheng)

Officially termed the Palace Museum (Gugong), the Forbidden City served for 500 years (until the end of the imperial era in 1911) as the source of all power in China, the throne of the Son of Heaven and the private residence of all the Ming and Qing dynasty emperors. Covering 74 hectares and containing some 800 individual buildings, the scale of the Forbidden City is hard to grasp, but visiting this monumental complex is an extraordinary experience.

Temple dogs abound in the Forbidden City

Although rebuilt and restored many times through the centuries, the structures of the Forbidden City retain the design and, above all, the impressive character of the originals. Begun in 1406 and completed in 1420, construction required the labours of 200,000 workmen. The earliest of the completely original structures date to the 18th century, the older structures having been destroyed by the frequent fires to which the wooden buildings were dangerously vulnerable, and the ravages of heavy-handed conquerors with a taste for pillage.

*Chang'an Ave. Entry is from Tiananmen Square, via the Tiananmen Gate and the Duanmen Gate to the entrance proper, which is at the Meridian Gate (Wumen). Tel: (010) 6513 2255, ext 615.*
*Open: Tue–Sun 8.30am–5pm (last entry at 3.30pm). Closed: Mon.*
*Admission charge (an excellent taped tour guide to the main locations is available for an extra charge).*

### Itinerary

The simplest way to tour the Forbidden City is to follow the central axis from south to north, over the Golden Stream, through the Gate of Supreme Harmony, and across the Sea of Flagstones, to the main ceremonial areas in the Hall of Supreme Harmony, the Hall of Complete Harmony, and the Hall of Preserving Harmony. Cross the Dragon Pavement to the imperial family's private domain, through the Gate of Heavenly Purity, to the Palace of Heavenly Purity, the Hall of Union, and the Palace of Earthly Tranquillity. Cross the Imperial Gardens to the Hall of Imperial Peace and the Gate of Obedience and Purity, exiting through the Gate of Divine Prowess. Along this principal route, visits can be made to the numerous side palaces and pavilions, many of which have been laid out as galleries and museums.

### Meridian Gate (Wumen)

This powerful defensive tower was built to guard the entrance to the Forbidden City. Today, it is where you buy your ticket to enter the main complex.

## Gate of Supreme Harmony (Taihemen)

This gate divides the ornamental outer courtyard, with its Golden Stream, from the more formal inner courtyard of the Forbidden City's ceremonial section. The courtyard beyond the gate could accommodate up to 100,000 people for imperial audiences.

## Hall of Supreme Harmony (Taihedian)

The most substantial of the official pavilions (28m high), this was also known as the Gold Throne Hall, and was used for important state occasions, for meetings with senior ministers, and for celebrating the emperor's birthday. Incense burners stand before the entrance, one in the shape of a stork, and another in the shape of a dragon;

both were auspicious symbols to an emperor. Numerous less ornate burners surround the building. Yellow tiles line the roof of the double-eaved structure, and rows of mythical animals, exquisitely rendered in miniature, face the corners. The tiled floor and gold-painted columns entwined with carved dragons are surmounted by a green-and gold-painted ceiling, littered with dragon motifs, from which hangs a spherical mirror. Beyond the Hall of Supreme Harmony's tourist-mobbed splendour, you must try to picture the majestic court rituals that took place here: the kowtowing courtiers in splendid robes, clouds of incense smoke, and above all the august figure of the emperor himself, presiding from the fantastically ornate Dragon Throne.

The Forbidden City is a vast complex of individual buildings and wide open spaces

## Hall of Complete Harmony (Zhonghedian)

Somewhat less formal than the Hall of Supreme Harmony and the Hall of Preserving Harmony, this elegant little square hall was used by the emperor as a resting point, and as a place for practising ceremonial speeches and actions. The dragons painted on the ceiling would have reminded officials that 'relaxation' was a relative term in the emperor's presence. Qing dynasty sedans, used for transporting the emperor around the palace, are on display.

## Hall of Preserving Harmony (Baohedian)

Highly decorated, and with ornate ceilings and beams, this graceful hall was used for imperial banquets, as a changing room for the emperor before official ceremonies, and as an examination centre for candidates for senior positions within the imperial bureaucracy. Behind the hall, a giant slab of marble, weighing more than 200 tonnes, is inscribed with dragon and cloud motifs.

## Gate of Heavenly Purity (Qianqingmen)

This marks the entrance to the inner sanctum, the palace area of the Forbidden City, which was accessible only to members of the imperial family.

Tortoise, symbol of longevity

## LESSER HALLS

The principal south–north route through the Forbidden City tells only a part of the story of this magnificent palace complex. Almost as impressive are the halls and gardens designed for day-to-day affairs of state, and for the imperial family's 'everyday life'.

Branching off to the east side, you will find several libraries and museums (including the Museum of Art Works Through the Dynasties), and numerous other palaces, pavilions and gardens (including the Palace of Prolonged Happiness, the Palace of Eternal Harmony, the Hall of Worshipping Ancestors, and the Hall of Imperial Supremacy). On the western side is another section of the Museum of Art Works Through the Dynasties, as well as the Hall of Mental Cultivation, the Palace of Peace and Tranquillity, and the Hall of Heroic Splendour.

The Hall of Supreme Harmony was used for formal functions

## Palace of Heavenly Purity (Qianqinggong)

Until the early 18th century, the emperors slept in this palace at the centre of the inner courtyard. After they withdrew to the Hall of Mental Cultivation, it was used to receive foreign ambassadors.

## Hall of Union (Jiataidian)

A water clock, or clepsydra, graces this small building, also known as the Hall of Vigorous Fertility. Here, the empress held court when the hall was used as living quarters by the imperial family.

## Palace of Earthly Tranquillity (Kunninggong)

During the Qing dynasty, this was the official residence of the empress, and the bedchamber for the imperial couple for several days following their nuptials. The garish red decoration of the

chamber put at least one emperor off his wedding-night ritual, so he and his new wife moved back to their permanent apartments.

## Imperial Garden (Yuhuayuan)

Located north of the Gate of Earthly Tranquillity, and around the Hall of Imperial Peace, the Imperial Garden seems surprisingly small – at least in comparison with the grandiose scale of the palace complex. Nevertheless, it covers some 7,000sq m in the classical Chinese garden style. Its impressive rock formations, pools and plant-bedecked spaces form a notable, and suitably tranquil, hideaway.

The footweary visitor will no doubt welcome a chance to rest here in the shade before leaving the Forbidden City through the Gate of Divine Prowess (also translated as the 'Gate of Divine Military Genius') which stands at the northern end of the complex.

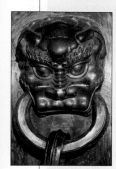

Beijing had its first taste of imperial glory in the 10th century as a secondary capital. Kublai Khan made it the primary one in 1279. Then, after a period during which Nanjing was the main city, Beijing again became the capital under the Ming emperor Yongle in 1420. After that, throughout the Ming and Qing dynasties, until 1911, the extravagance and power of the imperial court were still maintained in Beijing – the focal point of the Chinese empire.

Ensconced in the Forbidden City, the Son of Heaven became completely isolated, not only from his people, whom he viewed through a screen of Confucian duties, rituals, and displays of loyalty (and occasionally of rebellion), but often from reality itself. Throughout the Age of Enlightenment and the scientific revolution that was transforming Europe, China remained locked in a social system more appropriate to antiquity than to a great but now weakened empire, stalked by predatory foreign powers.

**Kowtowing Time**

On a visit to the Forbidden City, it takes considerable effort to shut out the noise of the chattering crowds, and to try to imagine the scene at one of the great court ceremonies of the past. The red walls and yellow-tiled roofs would then

Left and below: sections of the Forbidden City – silent reminders of a splendid past

have been veiled by swirling curtains of smoke from incense burners. Hosts of silk-clad officials would be kowtowing – kneeling with forehead touching the ground – as the emperor was carried in his palanquin to his magnificent throne. In the background would be gathered the 10,000 eunuchs and 9,000 ladies-in-waiting that the palace boasted at the height of its power. Such ceremonies continued to take place unchanged for five centuries, throughout the reigns of 24 emperors. Meanwhile, the world had changed, and Communism finally ruled in the imperial court. Whether they be antiquarians or tourists, Chinese or foreigners, all observers can be thankful that the people's government has finally opened the door on this venerable setting of Chinese mystery and intrigue.

Monsters line up on the Lama Temple roof
to ward off evil spirits

### Great Bell Temple
### (Dazhong Si)
The Great Bell Temple is appropriately
named, since it houses the biggest bell in
China, weighing almost 47 tonnes, and
covered in Buddhist scriptures. A special
canal had to be dug to move the bell to
its final home after it had been cast.
When winter came, the bell was loaded
on to a sledge and dragged over the
frozen canal surface.
*31A Beisanhuan Xi Rd. East of the
Friendship Hotel. Tel: (010) 6255 0843.
Open: daily 8.30am–4.30pm.
Admission charge.*

### Great Hall of the People
### (Renmin Dahui Tang)
China's parliament meets in this 1950s-
vintage edifice once a year in March to
consider the decisions of the Politburo
and Central Committee with great care,
before approving them. A guided tour
offers a glimpse of the style that the
people's tribunes have grown
accustomed to, including a 5,000-place
banqueting hall.
*Tiananmen Square. Tel: (010) 6309 6156.
West side of the square. Open: Mon–Sat
8.30am–2pm, except when official events
are taking place inside. Closed: Sun.
Admission charge.*

### Lama Temple (Yonghegong)
An extraordinarily large temple (the
biggest in Beijing), it owes its imposing
lines partly to its remodelling in 1694 to
serve as the residence of the future
emperor, Yongzheng. Today, it is an
important repository of Tibetan and
Mongolian Buddhist images and works
of art. The series of enclosures and
pavilions include a 26m-high statue of
the Maitreya Buddha, carved from a
single piece of sandalwood, the biggest
of many Buddha images inside.
*12 Yonghegong St. Tel: (010) 6404 3769.
Open: Tue–Sun 9am–4.30pm.
Closed: Mon. Admission charge.
Subway to Yonghegong station.*

### Mao Zedong Memorial Hall
### (Mao Zhuxi Jinian Tang)
Chairman Mao, the late Great
Helmsman of the People's Republic and
leader of the Chinese Revolution, is
embalmed here in a crystal sarcophagus.
Mao continues to command respect.

Despite the disasters he wrought, the official statistic that Mao was 70 per cent good and only 30 per cent bad still carries weight.

*Tiananmen Square. South side of the square. Tel: (010) 6513 2277. Open: daily 8.30–11.30am, Mon, Wed & Fri 2–4pm. Free admission.*

## Museum of the Chinese Revolution and Chinese History (Zhongguo Geming Lishi Bowuguan)

The museum building is a colossal tribute to the Socialist Realist school of architecture, dating from the late 1950s and early 1960s. The majestic sweep of Chinese history – from the time of Peking man, half a million years ago, through the imperial dynasties and up to 1919 – is covered in two sections of the museum. Another tells the story from 1919 and the foundation of the Chinese Communist Party; although less colourful, this is highly informative for anyone trying to understand the country today, and the many, often violent, transformations it has passed through.

*Tiananmen Square. East side of the square. Tel: (010) 6526 3355. Open: Tue–Sun 8.30am–5pm. Closed: Mon. Admission charge.*

## Museum of Natural History (Ziran Bowuguan)

This museum contains an impressive collection of flora and fauna, including a complete dinosaur skeleton, and a section on human evolution.

*126 Tianqiao Nan St. Just west of Tiantan Park. Tel: (010) 6702 4431. Open: Tue–Sun 8.30am–4pm. Closed: Mon. Admission charge.*

A place of reverence still: Mao Zedong's mausoleum and memorial hall

Scenes from Chinese history in the Long Corridor of the Summer Palace

## Old Summer Palace (Yuanmingyuan)

In 1860, European troops destroyed the buildings of the Old Summer Palace, originally laid out in the 12th century. Ironically, this gave Beijing one of its most beautiful sights, for at times when the Summer Palace is mobbed, the gardens of the old palace remain a sea of tranquillity. The 35sq km park has been afforested and some surviving architectural elements restored.
*Qinghua Xi Rd, Haidian District, north-western suburbs. Tel: (010) 6255 1488. Open: daily 7am–7pm. Admission charge.*

## Summer Palace (Yiheyuan)

The most magnificent of all China's royal gardens, the Summer Palace is an eloquent testimony to imperial power. Dowager Empress Cixi is credited with the palace's construction in 1888. She employed water as the principal motif, forming Kunming Lake in the process. The Long Corridor, stretching for 700m along the northern shore of Kunming Lake, commands superb views over the water and up to Longevity Hill. The interior is decorated with restored paintings of scenes from Chinese history. The Long Corridor leads to the Marble Boat of Cixi. Longevity Hill itself is studded with temples, pavilions, and pagodas, including the Temple of Scattering Clouds, the Temple of Buddhist Virtue, the Temple of Wisdom, the Hall of Virtuous Light, and the Repository of Sutras. On the eastern shore is the graceful 17-arch bridge that crosses to Nanhudao Islet.
*Haidian District, northwestern suburbs. Tel: (010) 6258 1144. Open: daily 9am–4pm. Admission charge.*

## Temple of Heaven Park (Tiantan Gongyuan)

Emperors of the Ming and Qing dynasties employed this evocative temple complex as a place to pray for good harvests. Like most imperial monuments, it is built on a vast scale. The 38-m high, blue-tiled roof of the Hall of Prayer for Good Harvests is a popular symbol of Beijing. Other notable features along the temple's main central axis are the Imperial Vault of Heaven, the Circular Altar, and the long flight of stairs connecting the temples.

*Tiantan Dong Rd. Southeast of the city centre. Tel: (010) 6702 2617. Open: daily 8am–5.30pm. Admission charge.*

## Tiananmen Gate (Tiananmen)

The Gate of Heavenly Peace dates from 1417 (restored in 1651). Today, its giant portrait of Chairman Mao is a familiar backdrop in images of the capital. This is the entrance to the Imperial City (although not to the Forbidden City proper), and only the emperor was permitted to use the central one of its five gates.

*Tiananmen Square. North end of the square. Tel: (010) 6513 2255, ext 615. Open: daily 8.30am–4.30pm. Admission charge to climb to the top of the gate. Free admission through the gate as far as the main entrance to the Forbidden City.*

### Other Parks

In addition to the parks described here, other valuable patches of green in Beijing are: Ditan Park, Grand View Garden, Honglingjin Park, Lido Park (swimming pool), Longtan Park, Ritan Park, Taoranting Park, Yuetan Park, Yuyuantan Park, Zhongshan Park, and Zizhuyuan Park.

## Tiananmen Square (Tiananmen Guangchang)

Laid out in 1959, Beijing's vast central square has witnessed gatherings of up to a million people, including the cheering throngs that were carefully trained to greet Chairman Mao's pronouncements. Since 1989, its name has been irrevocably associated with the pro-democracy demonstrations that ended in the Tiananmen Square Massacre and the subsequent suppression of the survivors. Mostly, however, it is a tranquil location to stroll in and watch people flying their home-made kites. At its southern end is the **Monument to the People's Heroes**, a 36-m high granite obelisk decorated with revolutionary images and calligraphy by Chairman Mao.

*Located immediately south of the Forbidden City.*

Temple of Heaven Park

# Beijing Environs

Some 580,000 years ago, the area around the town of Zhoukoudian, 50km southwest of Beijing, was occupied by a species of early proto-humans, whom palaeontologists have named Peking man. The first fossil was discovered in 1929 in a limestone cavern on Mount Longgu; since then, fragments of 40 other 'man-apes' have been uncovered in various locations.

Every province has its own specialised craft tradition

## Chengde

The resort town of Chengde is situated in the hills of Hebei Province, some 250km northeast of Beijing, about five hours away by train. Chengde's cool summer breezes led to the Imperial Summer Resort (Bishu Shanzuang) of the Qing Dynasty emperors being established here. This magnificent complex of gardens, lakes, bridges, pagodas, and palaces covers some 5.6sq km. The palace museum, in addition to rare jade and porcelain pieces, exhibits sedan chairs on which the emperors made the journey from Beijing. Among the notable buildings are the lakeside House of Mists and Rain (**Yan Yu Lou**), whose outlook seems like a ricepaper painting come to life, and a series of unusual Tibetan-inspired temples.
*Yan Yu Lou, located northwest of Chengde. Open: daily 8am–5pm. Admission charge.*

## Eastern Qing Tombs (Qing Dong Ling)

Among the notables entombed here are the Emperor Qianlong and the notorious Dowager Empress Cixi. Altogether, there are the tombs of five emperors, 14 empresses, and 130 or so other relations of the imperial families. The tombs of Qianlong and Cixi, although looted during the 1920s, still contain much of interest in the way of carvings, inscriptions, and other decorations.
*Zunhua County, 128km east of Beijing. Close to the Great Wall. Open: daily 8.30am–4.30pm. Admission charge.*

## Fragrant Hills (Xianshan Gongyuan)

This 150-hectare park is proof of Beijing's population explosion: on fine weekend days it will be jam-packed with people. Once a favoured retreat of

emperors, it reached its peak of popularity during the Qing dynasty under Emperor Qianlong, when it was known as the Garden of Tranquillity and Charm. The area is peppered with temples, pagodas, and pavilions, including the ruined Fragrant Hill Temple, the magnificent Luminous Temple with its Glazed Tile Pagoda, the Pavilion of Spacious Wind, and the Villa of Climbing to Clouds. The Temple of Azure Clouds (Biyun Si) contains the Hall of Five Hundred Arhats (508 representations of the Buddha), and the Diamond Throne Pagoda is surrounded by four smaller pagodas. A cable car travels to the summit of Incense Burner Peak, which gives a splendid view of the area.
*Western Hills. Can be reached by bus from the Summer Palace.*
*Tel: (010) 6259 1155. Open: daily*
*8am–5pm (until sunset in summer).*
*Admission charge.*

### Great Wall (Changcheng)
One of the greatest engineering feats of the ancient world, the Great Wall was begun in 221 BC by the Qin Emperor, Shi Huangdi, to protect China's northern frontier. It runs for 6,350km from Jiayuguan to Shanhaiguan. At restored sections, such as the one at Badaling, 72km northwest of Beijing, where the wall is 8m high and 6m wide, it winds spectacularly across the hills. Badaling can be oppressively busy, but most people give up after a short stroll, so one way of avoiding the crowds is to outwalk them.
*Badaling. Can be combined with a visit to the Ming Tombs. Tel: (010) 6912 1235.*
*Open: Mon–Fri 6am–6.30pm, Sat & Sun 6am–10pm. Admission charge.*

Universally known symbol of China, the Great Wall at Badaling

## Marco Polo Bridge (Lugouqiao)

Marco Polo may or may not have
personally seen the multi-arched Stone
Lion Bridge over Yongding River, dating
from 1189, but his is the name
permanently associated with it. It also
struck the imagination of the Qing
dynasty emperor, Qianlong, who
inspected the bridge and composed a
poem, *The Moon at Dawn Over Lugou*,
in its honour. A monument to the
emperor's inspection, with 485 carved
stone lions, stands at the western end of
the bridge.

*Wanping, 16km southwest of Beijing.*
*Tel: (010) 6381 5981. Open: 7am–7pm.*
*Admission charge.*

## Ming Tombs (Shisan Ling)

There are 13 Ming dynasty imperial
tombs in this 40sq km necropolis,
situated at the base of the optimistically
named Mountain of Heavenly
Longevity. Built between 1409 and 1644,
only three of the tombs are open to the
public, and only one, that of the 13th
Ming Emperor, Wanli, has been fully
excavated and laid out for visitors. While
the tombs themselves may sound
fascinating (inside they are mostly bare
underground vaults), they are reached
via the 7km Way of the Spirit, whose
first 750m, the Way of Stone Figures, is
guarded by two lines of fascinating stone
animals (some of them mythical), and

## Beijing Environs

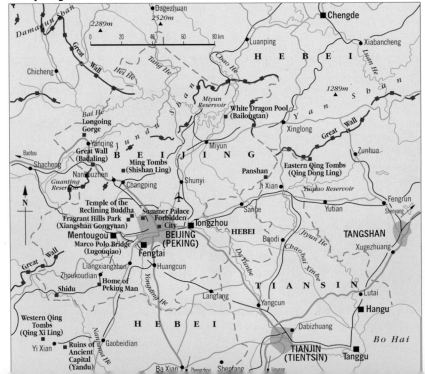

Popular weekend retreat from Beijing, the park surrounding the Ming Tombs

human servants of the emperor, all indicating respect for and loyalty to their departed master.
*Located 50km northwest of Beijing. Tel: (010) 6976 1424. Open: daily 8am–5.30pm. Admission charge. Often combined with a visit to the Great Wall.*

### Seaside Resorts
**Beidaihe**, six hours by train from Beijing, retains something of the air of a turn-of-the-century seaside town, but is very crowded. **Qingdao** has some of China's finest beaches.

### Temple of the Reclining Buddha (Wofo Si)
Also known as the Temple of Universal Spiritual Awakening, the building takes its name from the statue of the reclining or sleeping Buddha that it contains. Dating from 1331, it is the largest bronze statue in the country, more than 5m long and weighing 54 tonnes.
*Located between the Fragrant Hills and the Summer Palace. Tel: (010) 6259 1155. Open: daily 8am–4.30pm. Admission charge.*

### Western Qing Tombs (Qing Xi Ling)
The western burial ground of Qing dynasty emperors (1644–1911), who overthrew the Ming emperors, lies in the shadow of 1,121-m high Yunmeng Mountain, in rugged countryside 112km southwest of Beijing. The scenic outlook makes up at least in part for the fact that the tombs are fairly dull places to visit for all but an enthusiast for dead emperors. Only the tomb of the Emperor Guangxu, which dates from the early part of the 20th century, is presented to visitors.
*Beyond the town of Yi Xian. Open: daily 8am–4pm. Admission charge.*

# By Bike: Beijing

Because of the city's size, and the difficulties associated with public transport, the bicycle may be the most practical way of touring Beijing. Special cycle lanes make it generally safe, but great caution must be exercised at intersections and on roads without special lanes. An additional consideration is to secure the bike when you leave it (*see p182*).

*Allow 2 hours for this tour; longer if you want to explore the various locations en route.*

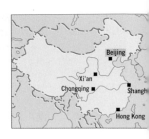

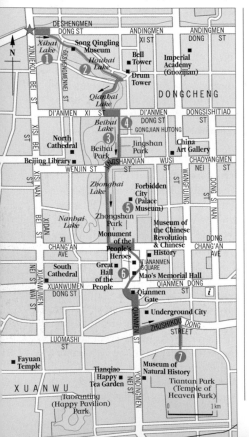

*Begin at the intersection of Xinjiekou Bei St and Deshengmen Dong St, then turn on to the Xihaibeiyan path along the north bank of Xihai Lake.*

## 1 Xihai Lake

This is the first in a series of lakes stretching southeast towards the city centre, forming a pleasant open space surrounded by *hutongs* (old neighbourhoods). Local people come here to fish, and compared with most of Beijing's public places, these lakes have a wild and ragged look which makes them all the more attractive.

*Cross Deshengmennei St and join the Houhaibeiyan pathway along the north shore of Houhai Lake.*

## 2 Houhai Lake

The tree-lined, rutted lakeside pathway is a bustle of *hutong* life and colour: students making for class, street traders, housewives with fresh fruit and vegetables, pungent cooking smells, and throngs of cyclists. Heavier traffic generally avoids this lane.

*Cross the stone bridge to the Qianhaibeiyan pathway along the western shore of Qianhai Lake, past the Lotus Flower street market. Then cross Di'anmen Xi St, and stop at the entrance to Beihai Park.*

## 3 Beihai Park

Bicycles are not permitted in the park, so leave yours at the stalls outside and explore the park on foot. This was formerly a playground of China's ruling women, favoured by the Dowager Empress Cixi, and by Jiang Qing, wife of Chairman Mao. Its highlights are **Jade Islet** and the **White Dagoba**.

*Return to Di'anmen Xi St and collect your bike. Cycle east a short way before turning right into the narrow lane through Gongjian Hutong.*

## 4 Gongjian Hutong

This offers a fascinating glimpse of Beijing as it used to be, away from the crowded apartment blocks taking over elsewhere. These small, tumbledown houses, all jumbled together, have an almost rural air.

*Emerging on Jingshan Xi St, take this narrow, busy road between Beihai Park and Jingshan Park, then on to Beichang St, then Nanchang St on the west side of the Palace Museum. Turn left into Tiananmen Square.*

## 5 Palace Museum

Tiananmen Gate, with its giant portrait of Chairman Mao, stands on the left, and through the gate is the entrance to the Forbidden City. This colossal monument to the glories of imperial China is worth an extensive visit, and is best tackled separately if time permits.

*Cross over into Tiananmen Square proper. Cycling is not permitted, so you must push your bike across it.*

## 6 Tiananmen Square

Passing the Great Hall of the People on your right and the Museum of the Chinese Revolution (*see p47*) on your left, you arrive across the vast expanse of the square to the Monument to the People's Heroes (*see p49*), and the Mao Zedong Memorial Hall (*see pp46–7*), where the embalmed body of the late leader is on display.

*Exit the square around the monumental Qianmen Gate at its southern end, into Qianmen St. Turn left into the Hutong district on Zhushikou Dong St, then right into Nanqiaowan St and Jinyuchizhong St, completing your tour at Tiantan Park.*

## 7 Tiantan Park

Cycles are not permitted in this 267-hectare monumental park which was sacred to the emperor as a centre of the state cult; he would come here each year to pray for a good harvest.

In China's crowded cities the bicycle is a reliable companion

# Chang Jiang (Yangtze River)

The longest river in China and third longest in the world, the Chang Jiang (Yangtze) is much more than a water course. Known as the Water of Gold, it flows through the geographical, spiritual, and historical heart of China.

From its source in the Tanggula Mountains of Qinghai Province, the river flows southeast through Tibet as the Tongtian, turns south, then north as the Jinsha, and becomes the Yangtze proper after Yibin in Sichuan. Here, it swings eastwards once again, crossing Hubei, Hunan, Jiangxi, Anhui and Jiangsu provinces to reach the East China Sea at Shanghai. Its source-to-mouth length is 6,300km.

The Yangtze river basin comprises an area of 1.8 million sq km – a quarter of China's cultivable land – and supports a vast population by providing irrigation and hydro-electric power. The river is also a major transport artery, navigable to ocean-going vessels for 1,000km, and to smaller vessels for 3,000km. Needless to say, it also serves as a convenient drain for the human and industrial wastes generated along its banks.

## CHONGQING

Chongqing is one of China's most beautifully located cities: it sits at the tip of a narrow peninsula in Sichuan province, where the Jialing and Yangtze rivers join in a natural amphitheatre formed by the surrounding hills. Sadly, despite its name (meaning 'Double Celebration'), the city does not match the drama of its situation, having been heavily bombed during World War II. Yet it has several points of interest, besides being the starting point for most downriver cruises on the Yangtze.

### Chaotianmen Dock

At the very tip of the peninsula on which Chongqing sits, the dock area offers a busy spectacle of barges and riverside life. Many (but not all) downriver cruises depart from here.
*Northern end of Xinhua Rd & Shaanxi Rd.*

### CABLE CARS ACROSS THE YANGTZE

Transportation facilities are notoriously overcrowded in China, but there seems to be something peculiarly claustrophobic about the two cable car systems that link Chongqing peninsula with the opposite banks of the Yangtze and Jialing rivers. Swinging precariously, the cars lunge across the yawning gap, with the muddy rivers rushing along beneath. The Yangtze cable car begins from a station off Xinhua Lu, and the Jialing from a station off Cangbai Lu. Daily: 6am–11pm. Fare charged.

## Chongqing Museum (Chongqing Bowuguan)

The museum contains remnants from ship burials, Han dynasty tombs, and dinosaur skeletons found near Chongqing.

*Pipashan Zheng Rd. Below Pipashan Hill.*
*Open: daily 8–11.30am & 2–5.30pm.*
*Admission charge.*

## Northern Hot Springs (Beiwenquan Gongyuan)

One of two thermal springs complexes near Chongqing, the Northern Hot Springs are set in a landscape of riverside hills. Visitors can bathe either in a public pool or private chambers. The springs are in a park which also features the Jinyun Temple (Jinyun Si), a Buddhist foundation dating to 1432.

*Beipei. Northwestern suburbs.*
*Open: daily 8am–6pm.*
*Admission charge.*

## Pipashan Park (Pipashan Gongyuan)

From its green eminence, high above the southern part of the Chongqing peninsula, the park commands a fine view over the Yangtze and the city. While there are some fairly rudimentary amusements and a few teahouses, as well as modern pavilions, Pipashan's big attraction is the chance it offers to rise above the gritty air of industrial Chongqing.

*Zhongshan Er Rd. Southwest of the city centre. Open: daily 6am–10pm.*
*Free admission.*

Food for free: fishing from the banks of the swirling Yangtze

## Daning River (Daning He)

The narrow but spectacular gorges of the Daning (*see p61*), a tributary of the Yangtze, are called the 'three lesser gorges', but what they lack in grandeur compared with their cousins on the main river (*facing page*) they certainly make up for in sheer drama. The sight of high-powered boats surging upstream against the current and churning past sections of rapids is not easily forgotten.

*These side-trips leave from Wushan (not to be confused with Wuhan!).*

## Dazu

A scenically situated town, 160km northwest of Chongqing, Dazu sits at the centre of one of China's most important Buddhist historical zones. The surrounding area is dotted with 50,000 stone carvings dating from the 9th to the 13th centuries AD, from the Tang to the Song dynasties. They can be found at 43 separate locations, the main groupings being at Baodingshan and Beishan. The Baodingshan group is based around a 12th-century monastery, and was originated by the monk, Zhou Zhifeng. His Sleeping Buddha is 31m high, and the Goddess of Mercy has 1,000 arms. The biggest single group is at **Beishan**, 2km north of Dazu. Among the 300 caves sunk into the cliffside there is a sculpture of Wei Junjing, the 9th-century warlord who became a famous stone sculptor.

Punishing the damned: carvings at Dazu

## YANGTZE MEGADAM PROJECT

In 1919 Dr Sun Yatsen, the founder of modern China, first suggested a dam 'to exploit the water resources' of the Yangtze River.

The megadam, known as the Three Gorges Project, and located upstream from Yichang, is on a scale that rivals the Great Wall. Foreign bankers estimate its cost will have reached US $70 billion by 2013. A 600sq km reservoir will be created, engulfing the gorges and 30,000 hectares of farmland. In the process more than a million residents will be relocated from 300 towns and villages along a 1,000-km stretch of the Yangtze.

There are serious concerns among environmentalists worldwide, who argue against the advantages of big dams, but supporters in China say it will improve flood control and irrigation, as well as supplying 10 per cent of China's total electricity needs.

Riding the rapids: heading up the Daning river gorge

## Three Gorges of Yangtze River

This is the high point of the Yangtze river cruises (*see p60*), as the wide swathe of the river narrows to hurtle through the gap between towering cliffs. At 8km in length, the **Qutang**, nicknamed the Windbox Gorge, is the shortest of the three gorges, but it offers a dramatic foretaste of what is to come. Downstream, beyond Wushan, Shennu Peak indicates the start of the 44km **Wuxia Gorge**, the most spectacular of the three, with six peaks lined up on each side of the river.

After a lengthy interval, the **Xiling Gorge** heaves into view beyond Zigui. At 75km, this is the longest (but also the least impressive) gorge, with rounded hills replacing the earlier jagged peaks.

## WUHAN

Most tour boats on the Yangtze begin or end their journey here at the capital of Hubei province, although some do so at the upstream port of Yueyang, or downstream at Shanghai.

## Guiyuan Temple (Guiyuan Si)

This Buddhist temple dates from the late Ming period and is one of the 10 biggest in China, noted for its 500 statues of the Buddha in the Hall of the Five Hundred Luohan.

*Cuiweiheng Rd. Open: daily 8.30am–5pm. Admission charge. South of Hanyang railway station.*

## Hubei Provincial Museum (Hubeisheng Bowuguan)

The archaeological collection includes 20,000 items excavated from the 2,400-year-old tomb of Marquis Yi, of Zeng in Suizhou, dating from the Warring States period. The tomb yielded a rich treasure of gold, jade, and bronze objects, and a fine set of 65 ceremonial bells.

*Donghu Rd. Beside East Lake (Dong Hu). Open: Tue–Sun 9am–5pm. Closed: Mon. Admission charge.*

# Cruise: Chang Jiang (Yangtze River)

A long, slow, lazy sail along the great riverine artery of central China. Tickets can be bought at Chongqing, although it makes sense to book through travel agents before you arrive. Different tour boats follow different itineraries and timings, although all follow the Yangtze on its course downstream (*see pp56–9*).
*Allow 3 days.*

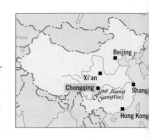

*Begin at Chongqing.*

## 1 Chongqing

An unremarkable, even ugly, city occupying a spectacular setting on a hilly peninsula at the confluence of the Yangtze and Jialing rivers which divides the city in three. Chongqing was the wartime capital of China's Kuomintang (Nationalist) government and suffered heavily from Japanese aerial bombardment. Boats leave from the Chaotianmen Dock passenger terminal at the peninsula's tip. The riverbank scene gives way slowly from urban to industrial to suburban, and finally to rural, with a hilltop pagoda seen outlined against the city skyline.
*The first downstream stop should be at Fengdu.*

## 2 Fengdu Ghost City

Ghost Mountain is the popular name for **Pingdushan Mountain**, which is dotted with temples and pavilions. These recall the legend of two men whose names, when joined together, became mistaken for that of the King of

Hell, and this reputation clung to the mountain down the centuries. Further on, a pagoda can be seen atop Shibaozhai rock on Jade Seal Hill. In addition to the rugged scenery along the banks, the river traffic ranging from tiny wooden junks to seagoing vessels, provides attraction enough. Fishing provides a livelihood for many inhabitants along the river.
*The boat should stop at Wanxian, where harbourside stalls serve meals.*

## 3 Yunyang Zhang Fei Temple

Lit by multicoloured lamps, at night the temple's narrow stairways, gloomy natural galleries, and legendary statues form a magical setting overlooking the river. Market stalls line the steep approach route, and thronging crowds may make the unbalustraded stairways hazardous.
*The boat should stop at Fengjie.*

## 4 Fengjie and Baidicheng 'White King' Town

Ancient capital of Kui during the Warring States period, Fengjie is a

pleasant enough town that displays little sign of its history now. Further on is Baidicheng, capital of the Western Han Dynasty's 'White King'.
*The boat now enters Qutang Gorge, first of the famous Three Gorges of the Yangtze.*

## 5 Qutang Gorge

Varying between 100–150m wide, the gorge funnels river, wind, and tour boat into a pell-mell rush between over-hanging hills. This is the most dramatic gorge with a 50m seasonal variation in the river's depth at this point.
*The boat may stop at Wushan, where passengers transfer to smaller craft for a side-trip along the Daning River.*

## 6 Daning River

The 'lesser gorges' of the Daning River are more spectacular than their bigger Yangtze cousins, as the water runs faster and the smaller boats come closer to the rocks and rapids. There are also some leisurely walks through riverside villages.
*The Yangtze tour boat continues through Wuxia and Xiling Gorges.*

## 7 Wuxia Gorge and Xiling Gorge

The drama factor reduces through these gorges, but the scenery is still memorable. At the end is the site of the great Yangtze Dam Project, which will eventually drown the gorges and a vast extent of land.
*Continue to Yueyang.*

## 8 Yueyang

The Yangtze is a sluggish creature by this time. Some tour boats end their journey here, allowing passengers to connect by rail at Changsha for the south. Yueyang is notable for its Tang-dynasty Yueyang Pavilion and the vast Dongting Lake.
*Continue to Wuhan.*

## 9 Wuhan

Most boats finish their trip here, although some continue as far as Shanghai. Wuhan is a big, industrial city notable for its Buddhist Guiyuan Temple, the 1,100-m long bridge over the Yangtze, and the Hubei Provincial Museum (*see p59*).

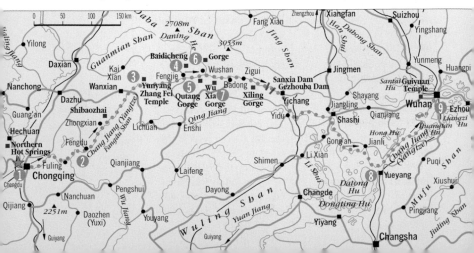

# Chengdu

Chengdu is the capital of Sichuan province, an area of west central China noted for its mild climate and fiery food, as well as for being the home of China's rare and endangered pandas. Chengdu's great moment in history passed more than 2,000 years ago: in the 4th century BC it was capital of the Kingdom of Zhou.

At the Baoguang Si Monastery

### Chengdu Zoo (Chengdu Dongwuyuan)

The main attraction of this rather miserable zoo is its collection of pandas, there being 12 on display. They, at least, have more space and greenery than the other 200 species of animals here, including rare golden-haired monkeys. Beside the giant panda enclosure is one for lesser red pandas, which seem more active than their cousins.

*Located 6km northeast of the city centre. Zhaojue Nan Rd, Chenghua.*
*Tel: (028) 351 9606.*
*Open: daily 8am–6pm.*
*Admission charge.*

### Monastery of Divine Light (Baoguang Si)

There has been a Buddhist monastery on this site for 1,900 years; earlier buildings were destroyed by war, and the present monastery was rebuilt in

1671. Its Tang Pagoda has 13 storeys, is 30m high, and has a pronounced lean. Other marvels are 500 representations of the Buddha, and the carved-stone Thousand Buddha Tablet which dates from AD 450.

*Xindu, 18km north of Chengdu.*
*Open: daily 8.30am–6pm.*
*Admission charge.*

### Mount Emei (Emeishan)

Chengdu is one of the bases from which to climb and explore this famed mountain some 140km southwest of the city.

### People's Park (Renmin Gongyuan)

The relaxed ambience and excellent tea served at the lakeside People's Teahouse (Renmin Chaguan) is one of the highlights of this city centre park. Chengdu is a relatively open and

## BY TRAIN FROM CHENGDU TO KUNMING

Few rail journeys can match the scenic splendour of the memorable 1,100km, 23-hour trip from Chengdu to Kunming.

As it makes its long, southerly swing through the mountains of Sichuan, the train traverses no fewer than 991 bridges and goes through 427 tunnels.

So many splendid views are there that the currency of splendour almost becomes devalued by the repetition of soaring mountains spanning the scenery and reaching into feathery white clouds, and steep descents into green valleys watered by plunging streams.

walkable city, but the park is still a welcome escape from traffic and crowds. *Chi Tang Ave, Shi Zhong Xin. Southwest of the city centre. Tel: (028) 613 0309. Open: daily 6.30am–midnight. Admission charge.*

### River Viewing Pavilion Park (Wangjiang Lou)

Part of the Brocade Riverside Park, the pavilion is dedicated to the Tang-dynasty poet, Xue Tao, who was fond of bamboo, which she regarded a symbol of modesty and self control. In her honour, the park hosts a renowned collection of more than 100 bamboo varieties from around the world. *Sichuan University campus. Southeastern sector of the city. Open: daily 6.30am–8pm. Admission charge.*

### Sichuan Provincial Museum (Sichuan Sheng Bowuguan)

The museum's exhibits cover the life and times of Sichuan, from murals and frescoes taken from ancient tombs, to mementoes recalling the progress of Mao Zedong's Long March through the province. Ming-dynasty calligraphy and painting is a speciality, and there are some spectacular bronze objects, including a tree with money hidden in the branches. *Renmin Nan Rd. At the junction with Nanyihuan Rd. Tel: (028) 522 2907. Open: daily 9am–5pm. Admission charge.*

### Temple of Marquis Wu (Wuhou Ci)

Also known as the Wuhou Temple, this is a wondrously vibrant place, with black-clad monks doing the

honours for the Marquis, whose real name was Zhu Geliang, an important statesman of the third-century Three Kingdoms period. *Wuhou Ci Da St. Adjacent to Nanjiao Park. Tel: (028) 555 2397/9027. Open: daily 8am–5pm. Admission charge.*

Buying mementoes at the Monastery of Divine Light

# Guangzhou (Canton)

The capital of Guangdong province is among the fastest growing cities on earth, in terms of population and wealth. The city is located in the Pearl River delta, close to Hong Kong, Macao, and their adjacent special economic zones. Western investment has flowed into the city from these capitalist neighbours, and the Cantonese, with their characteristic flair for business, have been quick to take advantage. On the downside, Guangzhou is busy, hot, preoccupied with making money, and is a magnet for unskilled peasants from the countryside migrating in search of a good life that many will never find.

## Conghua Hot Springs (Conghua Wenquan)

The mineral springs resort of Conghua lies in the hills some 80km northeast of Guangzhou, near the town of the same name. The temperature of the hottest spring is 70°C, and you can swim in or drink the waters in numerous hotels – the perfect way to cure the aches and pains induced by touring China. *The resort is 16km from Conghua, and can be reached by bus or taxi from the city.*

Popular culture: dragons in Guangzhou

## Cultural Park (Wenhua Gongyuan)

Sports and funfair attractions are featured in this popular centre which defines culture very broadly. Chinese Opera is occasionally performed here in full costume.

*37 Xi Ti Er Ma Rd. North of Shamian Island, near Renmin Bridge.*
*Tel: (020) 8188 2488.*
*Open: daily 8am–6pm & for performances. Admission charge.*

## Guangdong Provincial Museum (Guangdong Sheng Bowuguan)

Not nearly as impressive as most of China's provincial museums, the exhibits include some interesting archaeological objects, tools, and pottery from the Guangzhou region.

*Wenming Rd. South of the Pearl River.*
*Tel: (020) 8383 2195. Open: daily 9am–4.45pm. Admission charge.*

## Guangzhou Zoo (Guangzhou Dongwuyuan)

One of the largest in China – although not noticeably an improvement in terms of the space and facilities allotted to the animals – the zoo houses some 200 species, including pandas.

*Xianlie Zhong Rd. Tel: (020) 8775 5269.*
*Open: daily 8am–5pm. Admission charge.*

## Lotus Mountain (Lianhua Shan)

Not much of a mountain, really, but a fascinating and idyllic place nonetheless (except at weekends, when the crowds are out in force). This used to be a stone quarry, and weathered holes in the granite indicate where the stonemasons acquired the most impressive pieces. It became fashionable to inscribe calligraphy in the stone, and now gardens, lotus-filled pools, and viewing pavilions have been added to create a memorable stroll.

*Located some 40km southeast of Guangzhou, and reached by bus or boat.*
*Open: daily 8am–8pm.*
*Admission charge.*

Granite rocks encased in lush greenery provide a spectacular environment for walking enthusiasts in Lotus Mountains

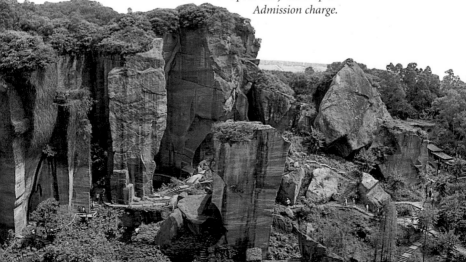

## Mausoleum of the 72 Martyrs (Huanghuagang Qishi'er Lieshi Mu)

This monument and park honours the first violent and unsuccessful attempt, led by Dr Sun Yatsen in 1911, to overthrow the Qing dynasty and drag China into the modern world. A later insurrection the same year was successful, and the monument was built in 1918 to commemorate the earlier

## Guangzhou

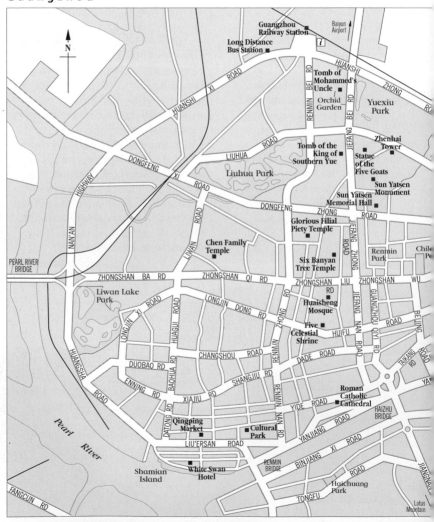

effort. Chinese people from around the world contributed to the cost, and had their names inscribed on the monument. A miniature representation of the Statue of Liberty symbolises the kind of democratic ideals espoused by Sun Yatsen and his followers, but lost sight of in the subsequent rise to power of the Communist Party.

*Xianlie Rd. On Yellow Flower Hill (Huanghua Gang).*
*Open: daily 9am–5pm.*
*Admission charge.*

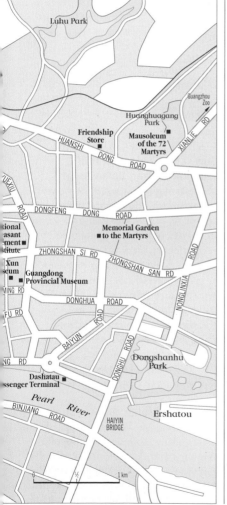

The Buddha of Guangzhou

Minute carvings on the Flower Pagoda, Six Banyan Temple

## CRUISING ON THE PEARL RIVER

As well as arriving in Guangzhou by boat, it is possible to make daytime and evening excursions on the Pearl River to view the fascinating life on the water, as well as the city's skyline. These leave from Pier No. 1, on the eastern side of Renmin Bridge and, in the evening, from nearby Pier No. 2, and from Shamian Island.

### Qingping Market (Qingping Shichang)

This big, shambolic, and for animal lovers, at any rate, potentially distressing market has become a tourist attraction in its own right since its opening in 1979. *Qingping Rd & Tiyun Rd, off Liu'ersan Rd.*

### Six Banyan Temple (Liu Rong Si Hua Ta)

Refreshingly, this temple is often filled with worshippers, and monks chant here on several mornings a week. The building takes its name from six banyan trees celebrated by the Tang-era poet, Su Dongpo, in the 11th century. The trees are no longer there. What remains is the nine-storey Flower Pagoda, almost 58m high, from which a superb view can be had over the old city. *Liurong Lu. City centre, west of Jiefang Zhong Lu. Tel: (020) 8339 2843. Open: daily 8am–6pm. Admission charge.*

### Sun Yatsen Memorial Hall (Sun Zhongshan Jinian Tang)

With seating for almost 5,000 people, this impressive theatre and cultural centre, set in spacious grounds, was built in honour of the mild-mannered revolutionary, Dr Sun Yatsen, who brought down the curtain on 5,000 years of imperial rule, and initiated republican government, in 1911. The hall hosts performances of music, theatre, Chinese opera, and dance. *Dongfeng Zhong Rd. North of the city centre. Tel: (020) 8355 2430. Open: daily & for performances. Admission charge.*

### White Cloud Hills (Baiyun Shan)

These green, lake-dotted hills, partly accessible by cable car, are a popular rambling and dining location with the Cantonese. Star Touching Hill is the highest. Although its summit is at the less-than-dizzy altitude of 380m, it still provides an extraordinarily fine view over the city and the Pearl River delta. *Northern suburbs of Guangzhou.*

**Yuexiu Park (Yuexiu Gongyuan)**
This 93-hectare park features the Beixu Lake, where rowing boats can be hired, a swimming pool, and other sports centres. The park also contains several monuments. These include the 28-m high Zhenhai Tower, which once formed part of the city wall and now houses a branch of the Guangdong Museum; a

sculpture of five rams representing the legend of Guangzhou's foundation by five gods who descended from heaven on rams to bring rice to the city; and the Sun Yatsen Monument, a granite obelisk dedicated to the founder of the Chinese republic, erected in 1929. Across Jiefang Bei Road at the front gate of the park is the Lanpu (Orchid Garden), with 10,000 examples of different orchid species. *Jiefang Bei Rd. Adjacent to the China Hotel. Tel: (020) 8669 0556. Open: daily 6.30am–8pm. Admission charge.*

Serene Buddha statues, inside the Six Banyan Temple

# Guilin

Located in the Guanxi Autonomous Region of southern China, Guilin has become one of the country's most visited cities, thanks to its setting in a landscape of limestone hills thrust up from the seabed 300 million years ago and immortalised in Chinese painting and poetry. The city itself, although pleasantly situated on the banks of the Li River and an attractive enough place for walking in, is busy, and its attractions are not quite as memorable as they are often made out to be.

BOAT TRIP ON THE LI RIVER

### Elephant Trunk Hill (Xiangbi Shan)

A much-photographed riverside rock formation at the junction of the Li and Yang rivers, it looks like an elephant drinking water. *Wenming Rd. Beside the river, south of the city centre, on the west bank. Tel: (0773) 282 5844. Open: daily 8am–5pm. Admission charge.*

### Folded Brocade Hill (Diecai Shan)

The Wind Cave en route to the top has Ming- and Song-era poetry inscribed on the walls, and Buddhist sculptures, some of them damaged by the Red Guards. The twin peaks of the 73-m high hill are named Bright Moon Crane and Seeing Around the Hill. Both offer views of

the city and the river. *Diecai Rd. Tel: (0773) 282 2762. Overlooking the river north of the centre, west bank. Open: daily 8am–6.30pm. Admission charge.*

### Reed Flute Cave (Ludi Yan)

The stalagmites and stalactites of this cave are magically lit, and present an extraordinary underground vista. The great limestone galleries lead to petrified accretions that have adopted fantastical shapes over the millennia. All have names, and some of them are clearly as described, while others are fanciful or depend on poetic licence. *Ludi Rd, at Yujiazhang. Several km outside town, to the northwest. Bus 3 from*

There can be no better way of viewing the stunning limestone hills around Guilin than from the deck of one of the small cruise boats that make the 8-hour journey from the city downstream to Yangshuo (although if time permits, going there by mountain bike is also good). The boat offers a close-up view of the strange rock formations that give this area a feeling of 'the land that time forgot'. Life on the river is equally fascinating, with fishermen on bamboo rafts using cormorants to bring in the catch. Traders on flimsy rafts manoeuvre alongside the rapidly moving excursion boats in a dangerous sales tactic, offering fruit and T-shirts.

*Guilin railway station.*
*Tel: (0773) 282 2254. Open: daily 8am–*
*4.40pm. Admission charge.*

## Seven Star Park (Qixing Gongyuan)
The park gets its name from its peaks being aligned more or less in the same configuration as the stars of the Plough in the Ursa Major (Great Bear) constellation. Adjacent to the park are stone stelae (standing stones) carved with calligraphy at the Guilin Forest of Stone Inscriptions. The sad-looking Guilin Zoo is also here.
*Ziyou Rd. East bank of the river, beyond*
*Liberation Bridge. Tel: (0773) 581 4342.*
*Open: daily 8am–5pm. Admission charge.*

## Yangshuo
Yangshuo is where cruises downriver from Guilin finish. The town has the same advantages as Guilin, in terms of its location among the limestone hills, but without the hassles, hype, and overcharging of that city. The Yangshuo waterfront, however, is a noisy tourist-trap of souvenir stalls and photogenic cormorant fishermen who want payment for pictures taken. Away from the riverside, the village lives up to its 'more genuine' reputation, and is a good place for strolling around.
*On the Li River, some 80km south of*
*Guilin. The bus from Guilin takes less*
*than 2 hours.*

Like scenes from a Chinese painting, the hills of Guilin

# R u r a l   L i f e

A tour bus arrives at a tea-producing village. Its occupants have been told that they will learn about life in the countryside, the care lavished on the tea plants, and the venerable Chinese tea ceremony. Instead, the bus is ambushed by hollering villagers who grapple with the passengers, trying to force bags of tea on them in return for cash. After a few minutes, the shaken tourists retreat to the bus, which then leaves. Little of cultural value has been exchanged, nor has much tea been sold.

Not all slices of country life are like this, but it is indicative of a common attitude in a society that was once egalitarian in its deprivation, and which now sees the chance to grab prosperity with both hands. The countryside

was first to benefit from the open-market reforms introduced by Deng Xiaoping. Communes, production brigades, collectivisation – the paraphernalia of a centralised command economy was dismantled, and peasants were allowed to make money for themselves instead of mouthing slogans.

## Hidden World

This undoubtedly makes them happy, although it is hard to tell. Most visitors pass through China without the slightest notion of what goes on in the countryside – apart from an occasional glimpse of farmers ploughing with their buffaloes, or families working in the paddy fields. The countryside is China's big mystery, a reservoir of resentments and unknowns that remains an enigma even to the Communist Party elite in Beijing: China's rulers know that long-suffering peasants have always provided the foot soldiers of rebellion. As far as anyone can tell, however, the billion or so peasants are too busy saving for 'DVD players or mobile phones' to worry about revolution at the moment, and life in the countryside has advantages over that in crowded, polluted cities. Yet an estimated 150 million peasants are on the move, searching for work. Many can be seen sleeping on the pavement outside railway stations. That, too, has become a part of country life.

Men and women both work in the fields, pursue rural crafts, and carry their produce to sell in the city

# Hangzhou

Capital of Zhejiang province, Hangzhou was also made capital of China in 1127 during the reign of the Song-dynasty Emperor Gaozong, who was captivated by the beauty of the city's West Lake. It is indeed a pearl beyond price, although in danger of being dulled by too much lakeside development. Just two hours by train from heavily populated Shanghai, Hangzhou can get crowded, and many of its finest sights are immersed in a cataract of noise from tourists and the battery-powered loudhailers used by tour guides. This is sad, because Hangzhou deserves to be savoured.

### Grand Canal (Da Yunhe)
The southern terminus of the 1,800-km long Grand Canal can be seen in Hangzhou's northern and eastern reaches, along Huancheng Bei Road and Huancheng Dong Road.

### Peak that Flew from Afar (Feilai Feng)
The rock formations of this hill, which legend says flew to China from India, are carved with 380 sculptures dating from the 10th to the 14th centuries, of which the most important is that of the Laughing Buddha.
*Lingyin Rd. Adjacent to the Temple of Spiritual Retreat. Open: daily 8am–6pm.*
*Admission charge.*

### Precious Stone Hill (Baoshi Shan)
The most notable feature of the hill is the Baochu Pagoda (Baochu Ta), originally built in the 10th century for the safe return of the Tang Prince Chu, but unattractively restored in the 1930s. The wooded hill overlooks West Lake.
*Off Baishan Rd. North shore of West Lake.*
*Open: daily 8am–6pm.*
*Admission charge.*

### Temple of Spiritual Retreat (Lingyin Si)
Saved from destruction during the Cultural Revolution only by the personal intervention of Premier Zhou Enlai, this beautiful temple dates originally from AD 326,

## THE GRAND CANAL

Two boats a day sail between Hangzhou and Suzhou (*see p108*) – a taste of pre-railway days when the Grand Canal (*see pp114–15*) was the only viable means of long-distance transport in this area. Emperors and their courts used the canal, as did ordinary people for transporting themselves and their goods. Barges still transport goods on the Grand Canal, but nowadays only tourists move on the water with the leisure of former days. Boats leave from the Hangzhou Passenger Wharf on Huancheng Beilu, about 1km east of the long-distance bus station.

although the structure has been rebuilt many times since then. A 24-m high camphor-wood statue of the Buddha is the highlight of the Temple, located in the Great Hall.

*Lingyin Rd. Located 3km inland from the western shore of West Lake. Open: daily 9am–6pm. Admission charge.*

## West Lake (Xihu)

First by far among Hangzhou's many attractions is the magnificent West Lake, around which the city has been built. Dozens of scenic spots dot its shores, waters, and islands. Many have poetic names, such as Autumn Moon Over the Calm Lake, Three Pools Mirroring the Moon, Solitary Hill, and Watching Goldfish at Flower Harbour. Part of the lake's charm is the chance to slip into the poetic appreciation of nature that was once the hallmark of China's leisured classes. Sadly, this is not always possible due to the throngs of visitors and a seemingly inexhaustible supply of noise. Nevertheless, West Lake is just about big enough to find places where visitors can escape for peace and quiet.

Pleasure boats leave from various points on excursions across the lake, which covers about 9sq km, and gondolas can also be hired with an oarsman for a slower but more individual appreciation of the sights. The gardens, pools, and zigzag bridges of Santanyinyue and Xiaoyingzhou islands (in the southern part of the lake) are among the most popular beauty spots.

The Laughing Buddha, on the Peak that Flew from Afar

# Hong Kong and Macao

Ancient and modern in Macao

## Hong Kong

Formerly a British Crown Colony, this fast-paced city-state has one of the world's most vibrant economies. On 1 July 1997, Hong Kong returned to Chinese rule, ending a connection that went back to 1841, when Britain seized Hong Kong Island, it being formally ceded the following year. In 1860, the mainland territory of Kowloon was also ceded to Britain, and in 1898, the New Territories, Lantau Island, and other outlying islands were leased for 99 years. China's 'one country; two systems' proposal should allow Hong Kong a large degree of independence in domestic affairs. Its free port and customs status is being retained, and the Hong Kong dollar (HK$) remains the official currency.

Hong Kong lies off the southeastern coast of China. The territory consists of Hong Kong Island, Kowloon, and the New Territories, along with some 230 islands and islets. With a population of almost 6 million living in just over 1,000sq km, it is notoriously densely populated. Just northeast of the territory is the booming Shenzhen Special Economic Zone, created as a part of China's plan to benefit from Hong Kong's economy.

### Hong Kong

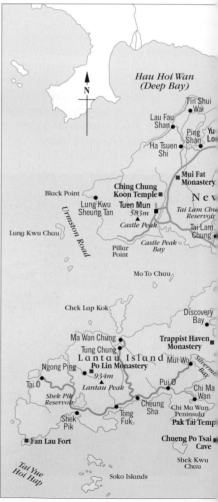

## Macao

Formerly a Chinese territory under Portuguese administration, Macao lies some 60km west of Hong Kong. Portuguese settlement in Macao dates from 1557, although the right of permanent occupation was only granted to Portugal in 1887, and the territory returned to Chinese sovereignty in 1999. The territory includes the islands of Taipa and Coloane, which are reached by bridge from Macao town.

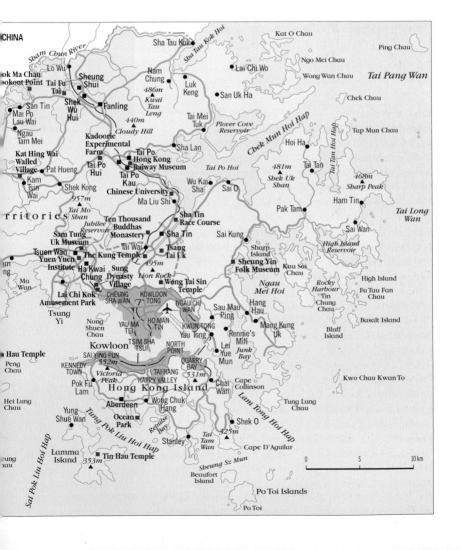

# Hong Kong Island

The attractions of the island are endless. Hong Kong's financial centre is here, along with an antiques and curios district, ferry terminals for the islands, beaches and coastal resorts, the Wanchai nightclub area, Victoria Peak (reached by a hillside tram), and some fabulous shopping, dining, and entertainment possibilities. Getting about is easy using either the bus system or the metro (known as the MTR – the Mass Transit Railway).

## Bays and Beaches

The island's south coast is dotted with resorts and some fine beaches, although the resorts can be pretty crowded, and typical Hong Kong tower blocks are never far from view. In addition, the water is polluted enough to make one think twice about stepping into the invitingly azure sea. The fishing port of Aberdeen, with its junk-crowded harbour and floating restaurants, is a picturesque sight, and nearby are the Ocean World aquatic theme park, the beaches of **Repulse Bay**, and the coves of Stanley, also noted for its market. *The south coast resorts and beaches are reached by bus from the underground station at Exchange Square, between the Star Ferry and the Vehicular Ferry Pier.*

## Fung Ping Shan Museum

This museum contains a good display of Chinese art, organised chrono-logically, so that it acts as a good introduction to the bronze, ceramics, and painting exhibits. There is also a very unusual collection of bronze crosses from the Yuan Dynasty (1279–1368). *94 Bonham Rd, University of Hong Kong. Tel: (0852) 2241 5500. Open: Mon–Sat 9.30am–6pm. Closed: Sun. Free admission. Bus 3 to Bonham Rd.*

## Hong Kong Park

This beautifully designed oasis of green has fountains and pools, an aviary, a greenhouse, a visual arts centre, an amphitheatre, and *tai chi* exercises in the mornings.

## LANTAU

Lantau, Hong Kong's largest island (larger, in fact, than Hong Kong itself), lies an hour away by ferry from Central. The ferry calls at several smaller islands before reaching the main Lantau Harbour, Silvermine Bay (Mui Wo). Lantau is a weekend retreat. Hong Kongers go to climb the 943m Lantau Peak, visit **Po Lin (Precious Lotus) Monastery**, with its 34m statue of the Buddha, or to explore **Tai O**, a fishing village on stilts. There is now a new airport on Lantau's northern coast.

In addition, there is all-important shade and fragrant air. The excellent **Museum of Tea Ware** is located inside the park.
*Main park entrance: Supreme Court Rd. Tel: (0852) 2530 0154. Open: daily 7am–11pm. Free admission. Museum of Tea Ware. Tel: (0852) 2530 0154. Open: Thu–Tue 10am–5pm. Closed: Wed. Free admission. MTR station: Admiralty.*

### Man Mo Temple

Dedicated to an unlikely combination of the calligraphy-creating God of Literature and the sword-bearing God of War, this large Taoist temple is an important religious foundation dating from the early years of British rule, and situated next to the steeply rising staircase of Ladder Street.
*Hollywood Rd. Mid-Levels. Open: daily 7am–5pm. Free admission.*

### Tiger Balm Gardens

Also known as the Aw Boon Haw Gardens, this theme park of pagodas, grottoes, and scenes from Chinese folktales and legends was founded by Aw Boon Haw, who made his fortune from inventing Tiger Balm, the cure-all ointment used all over Asia.
*Tai Hang Rd. South of Causeway Bay. Open: daily 9.30am–4pm. Free admission.*

### Victoria Peak

The spectacular view of Hong Kong from the top of Victoria Peak would be reason enough to make the journey, but getting there by the Peak Tram railway makes the experience doubly entertaining. Once there, a curious fountain with dancing water-jets, and an up-market shopping gallery are about the only attractions, although you can follow the tarmac-covered path all the way round the peak for dizzying views in every direction.
*Garden Rd. The Peak Tram operates daily between 9am & 10pm. Tel: (0852) 2489 0668. Ticket charge. Station adjacent to the US Consulate.*

Junk and junks in Aberdeen Harbour, on the south side of Hong Kong Island

# KOWLOON

Kowloon occupies the southern tip of the Chinese mainland, facing Hong Kong Island's northern shore. Traditionally more of a dormitory zone for the business districts on Hong Kong Island, it has developed as an industrial (and now a shopping) centre in its own right.

## Kowloon Park

This glorious green, shaded, and ornamented park, in the heart of downtown Kowloon, has lakes, flower gardens, children's playgrounds, an outdoor art gallery called the Sculpture Walk, and an indoor sports complex. The Hong Kong Mosque stands in the southeast corner of the park.
*22 Austin Rd, between Nathan Rd & Kowloon Park Drive. Tel: (0852) 2724 3344. Open: daily 6am–midnight. Free admission.*
*Nearest MTR station: Tsim Sha Tsui.*

## Museum of Art

The museum's six exhibition galleries contain a fine selection of historical and contemporary Chinese art, including lithographs of old Hong Kong. Visiting exhibitions from around the world vary the programme, but the emphasis is on Chinese antiquities, fine arts, historic Hong Kong and contemporary works by Hong Kong artists. One gallery contains the Xubaizhai collection of historic Chinese painting and calligraphy.
*Cultural Centre, 10 Salisbury Rd, Tsim Sha Tsui. Adjacent to the Star Ferry terminal on Kowloon side. Tel: (0852) 2734 2167. Open: Mon–Wed, Fri & Sat 10am–6pm, Sun 1–6pm. Closed: Thu. Admission charge.*

## Museum of History

This excellent museum traces 6,000 years of Hong Kong history, from the earliest traces of human habitation, through the many dynasties of China, to the foundation of the British colony and Hong Kong's subsequent development to become one of the world's most fascinating cities.
Highlights are the archaeological finds from Tang-dynasty kilns, and Song- and Ming-dynasty villages.
*Kowloon Park, 100 Chatham Rd, Tsim Sha Tsui. Tel: (0852) 2724 9042. Open: Tue-Sat 10am–6pm, Sun 1–6pm. Closed: Mon. Admission charge. Nearest MTR station: Tsim Sha Tsui.*

## Sung Dynasty Village

Despite the somewhat tacky and Disneyesque rendition of Chinese life and culture during the Sung (or Song) dynasty (AD 960–1279), this still succeeds in being fairly charming and interesting. Fortune-telling, martial arts displays, woodcarving, tea-making, marriage ceremonies, and other traditional crafts and activities are represented by performers wearing traditional costume.
*Kau Wah Keng, Lai Chi Kok. Open: daily 10am–8.30pm. Admission charge. Nearest MTR station: Mei Foo. Bus 6A from the Star Ferry terminal.*

## Waterfront Promenade

The colonnaded and traffic-free walkway, shaded from the sun, runs alongside Kowloon Public Pier, past the Clock Tower, the gracefully modern buildings of the Hong Kong Cultural Centre, and the Space Theatre. It is a

pleasant place to stroll at any time. It is also a popular place to sit and watch the busy harbour full of ships, from junks to ocean-going tankers, as it offers an excellent vantage point for the glittering night-time view of Hong Kong Island across the water.
*Adjacent to the Star Ferry terminal on Kowloon side.*

### NEW TERRITORIES

The New Territories occupy a great swathe of mostly rugged territory between Kowloon and the Chinese border. Although parts are being filled in by fast-growing new towns, the New Territories retain much that is wild and natural, astonishingly so with Hong Kong so near.

Among the attractions in this area are Lau Fau Shan, a village on the northwest coast noted for its oysters (both their production and consumption); the Maclehose Trail, a long-distance footpath on the Tai Mo Shan Mountain; the Mai Po Marshes, a notable spot for birdwatching on the northwest coast; and the **Yuen Yuen Institute**, a temple complex in which Buddhism, Taoism, and Confucianism are represented, as well as a replica of Beijing's Temple of Heaven.

If you lack your own transport, consider exploring the New Territories with one of the guided tours offered by the HKTA (Hong Kong Tourist Association). *Toll-free tel: (800) 282 4582. www.discoverhongkong.com*

Attractive packaging even of fresh foods is a speciality of the shopping mecca that is Hong Kong

## MACAO

The Portuguese settled in Macao during the mid-1550s. Today, 95 per cent of its population is Cantonese-speaking Chinese. The remainder is mostly Portuguese, with a sprinkling of other foreign nationals. A reclamation project is under way to convert Taipa and Coloane Islands into one island, making space for the new Macao International Airport and increasing the territory's land area by 20 per cent.

### Church of São Paulo

The fine Baroque façade and stairway are all that remain of this 17th-century Catholic church. Built between 1602 and 1637 with the help of Japanese Christians, who had fled persecution in Nagasaki, it was all but destroyed by a fire in 1835.
*Rua da Ressurreicao. City centre, adjacent to the Citadel of São Paulo do Monte. Free admission.*

### Citadel of São Paulo do Monte

Also known as the Monte Fort, the powerful defensive Citadel of Macao was built between 1617 and 1626, and was responsible for the defeat of a Dutch invasion force in 1622. It now houses the Macao Weather Observatory, and offers fine views over the town and to China, across the Pearl River.
*Travessa dos Artilheiros. City centre, adjacent to the Church of São Paulo. Tel: (0853) 363 057. Open: daily 7am–6pm. Free admission.*

### Coloane Park

Covering 20 hectares, the gardens are wonderfully colourful, with a wide range

The façade of São Paulo's Baroque church

of trees, flowers, and plants, as well as ponds and a walk-in aviary.
*Coloane Island. Near the Taipa–Coloane causeway. Tel: (0853) 870 295. Open: daily 9am–7pm. Free admission. Bus: 21A from Macao.*

### Guia Fortress

Dominating the highest point in Macao, this fort sits atop the green and tranquil Guia Hill. Among the old cannon-dotted walls, which date from the 1630s, are a lighthouse and a small church. The lighthouse dates from 1865, and is the oldest on the Chinese shoreline.
*Colina da Guia. Above the Hong Kong-Macao Ferry Terminal. Tel: (0853) 569 808. Open: daily 9am–5.30pm. Free admission.*

### Kun Iam Tong Temple

The 360-year-old Ming-dynasty Buddhist temple is dedicated to the Queen of Heaven and the Goddess of Mercy. It is the largest temple in Macao, and around one of its altars are three gold-lacquered statues of the Buddha. In the garden is the Lover's Tree which, according to legend, arose on the spot where a suicide pact was observed by two young lovers.

*Avenida do Coronel Mesquita. Macao town centre. Tel: (0853) 556 127. Open: daily 7am–6pm. Free admission.*

## Leal Senado (Municipal Council)

The Loyal Senate House dates from 1784, and contains a stone tablet, inscribed in Portuguese, describing Macao as the 'City of the name of God, Macao, there is none more loyal' because it remained loyal to Portugal when the home country was occupied by the Habsburgs.

*Largo do Senado. Macao town centre. Tel: (0853) 387 333. Open: Mon–Sat 1–7pm. Closed: Sun. Free admission.*

## Taipa House Museum

A new museum housed in one of the old Portuguese colonial villas in Taipa village, this is devoted to exhibiting the old style of life in the territory.

*Taipa Praia. Near the Taipa–Coloane causeway. Tel: (0853) 827 088. Open: Tue–Sun 9.30am–1pm & 3–5.30pm. Free admission.*

### Gambling in Macao

A third of Macao's revenues come from gambling, conducted in a constellation of eight casinos operated under a government franchise by a local business syndicate. Masses of slot machines can be played alongside Western casino games such as blackjack, baccarat and roulette, as well as such popular Chinese ones as *fan tan*, *dai siu* (big-small), *pai ko,* and *keno*. In addition, there is dog-racing at the Canidrome and horse-racing at the Macao Jockey Club's racetrack on Taipa island.

Sino-Portuguese shop-houses in Macao's main square

# Tour: Hong Kong by Public Transport

This tour focuses on the heart of Hong Kong, around the harbour, and takes full advantage of the remarkable efficiency and frequency of service offered by its cheap public transport network, both on land and water.

*Allow 4 hours.*

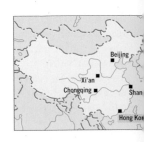

*Begin on Hong Kong Island at the Star Ferry Pier in Central.*

## 1 Star Ferry to Kowloon

The busy ferries, painted green and white, are a popular symbol of Hong Kong and are among the city's joys. For a fare of almost nothing, they afford a ringside view of **Victoria Harbour**, one of the world's most fascinating and animated waterfront scenes, as well as of the serried ranks of skyscrapers on either shore.

*Turn right from the Star Ferry Pier on the Kowloon side.*

## 2 Kowloon Public Pier

A short detour on the elegantly modern peristyle walkway, beside the waterfront, leads past the venerable Clock Tower, the Hong Kong Cultural Centre, and the Space Theatre, then past the stellar Peninsula Hotel to the bus terminal in front of the Star Ferry Pier.

*Take bus No. 1, 1A, 2, 6, 6A, or 9.*

## 3 Nathan Road

Get off the bus at the Tsim Sha Tsui MTR station beside the mosque on Nathan Road. A little beyond the mosque is the entrance to Kowloon Park *(see p80)*; enter for a stroll around this green, scented garden. Return to Nathan Road beyond the Park Lane Shoppers Boulevard, a shopper's paradise – or nightmare, if 'shop-until-you-drop' is not your idea of time well spent.

*Take any of the northbound buses and get off at the junction of Nathan Rd & Waterloo Rd. Change to a westbound No. 7 bus for the Jordan Rd Vehicular Ferry Pier.*

## 4 Central-Jordan Road Ferry

The ferry takes you back across the harbour, this time on a less stylish ferry, but one whose view is no less memorable.

*Cross Connaught Rd Central via the footbridge, and follow Jubilee St to Des Voeux Rd Central.*

## 5 Mid-Levels Hillside Escalator

At 800m, the world's longest escalator ascends the steep hillside among shops, houses, and restaurants. However, as the escalator goes only in one direction at a time (upwards from 10.30am to 10pm), it may be wise not to venture too far as you will have to return on foot.

*Return to Des Voeux Rd Central and take any eastbound tram. Get off in front of*

Chater Garden. Walk up Garden Rd to the Peak Tram station.

## 6  The Peak Tram

The tram glides uphill through rugged scenery to the finest view in Hong Kong, and to another good shopping centre.
*Return on the Peak Tram and thence to Des Voeux Rd Central. Then take any eastbound tram. Get off at Hong Kong Park.*

## 7  Hong Kong Park

This fulfils the same oxygen-giving function on this side of the water as Kowloon Park on the opposite shore, as well as being a place for early-morning

*tai chi* exercises.
*Return to the tram line on Queensway and take any eastbound tram. Get off at Pacific Place.*

## 8  Pacific Place

Shopping is Hong Kong's top participatory sport, and the Pacific Place Shopping Mall is one of the principal venues, with many of the big names represented, and some excellent restaurants.
*Return to Queensway and take any eastbound tram. Get off at the junction of Johnston Rd and Hennessy Rd. Either walk or take a taxi the short distance north to return to the Wanchai Ferry Pier.*

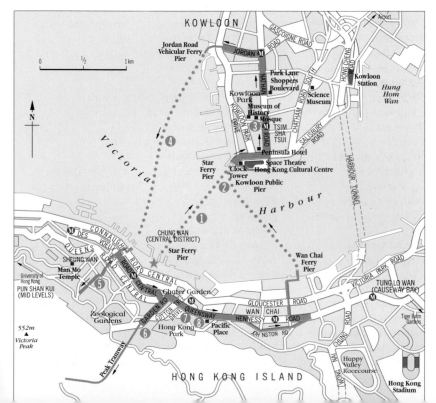

# Huang He (Yellow River)

China's second-longest river, the Huang He, rises in the Bayar Shan mountains of Qinghai and flows through Inner Mongolia before snaking across northern central China, covering a total of 5,500km on its journey to the Bo Hai Gulf, southeast of Tianjin. Earlier known as 'China's Sorrow' because of its tendency to produce drastic floods, its negative impact has been reduced by dykes and other control measures. There are a number of interesting towns along its banks.

## JINAN

Renowned as the City of Springs, the capital of Shandong province was founded in the 8th century BC and flourished as a commercial centre during the Tang dynasty (AD 618–907). It is 15km from the south bank of the Yellow River on the Beijing–Shanghai railway line. Its springs are not as impressive as they used to be, as a result of lower water levels in the underground aquifers.

### Black Tiger Spring (Heihuquan)

The water originates in a cave at this park, and surges out of the mouths of three stone tigers in an area where many other springs emerge.
*Heihuquan Rd. East of the city centre. Open: daily 8am–5pm. Admission charge.*

### Daming Lake (Daming Hu)

Weeping willows, gardens, playgrounds, teahouses, and pavilions adorn the banks of the 'Lake of Great Brightness', which suffers from the same lowered water table that affects Jinan's springs. Nevertheless, this is a welcome stretch of greenery and cool water in the heart of the city.
*Daminghu Rd. South of the Jinan-Qingdao railway line. Open: daily 8am–8pm. Admission charge.*

### Jet Spring (Baotu Quan)

Also translated as the 'Gushing from the Ground Spring', its waters emerge

## QUFU: BIRTHPLACE OF CONFUCIUS

Qufu, 150km south of Jinan, is an attractive small town and an emblematic spot as the birthplace of Confucius (Kong Fuzi), the most influential of China's ancient sages. He lived from 551 to 447 BC, during the time of warfare and political upheavals known as the Spring and Autumn Period. He proposed a return to order by means of strict adherence to traditional precepts of correct behaviour at all levels of society. Among the many Confucian sites in Qufu, the most significant are the Tomb of Confucius (Kong Ling), the Confucian Temple (Kong Miao), the Dacheng Hall (Dacheng Tang), and the Kong Family Mansion (Kong Fu).

in a pond by means of three fountains out of a total of 16 in the gardens in which the spring is set. This spring is framed by pavilions, including the Song-dynasty Source of the Luo Hall (Luoyuan Tang), and the Wave-Viewing Pavilion (Guanlian Ting).

*Baotuquan Rd. Adjacent to the city moat. Open: daily 8am–5pm. Admission charge.*

### Shandong Provincial Museum (Shandong Sheng Bowuguan)

Moved from its former city-centre site, this museum still features an extensive collection of archaeological finds, including frescoes, Buddhist sculptures, musical instruments, and tomb ornaments. Its most important single exhibit is a 4,000-year-old collection of Longshan black pottery. A 2,000-year-old treatise on the art of war, written on bamboo strips, is also on display.

*Qianfoshan Rd. Adjacent to Thousand Buddha Mountain. Tel: (0531) 2967179. Open: Tue–Sun 9am–5pm. Closed: Mon. Admission charge.*

### Taishan Holy Mountain (Taishan)

One of China's five sacred mountains, (*see pp128–9*) Taishan is 50km south of Jinan.

### Thousand Buddha Mountain (Qianfoshan)

Buddhist images are carved into the cliffside here. At the top of a steep climb is the Temple of the Flourishing State (Xingguo Si), with about 60 Buddha images ranging in height from 20cm to more than 3m, dating from the 6th century AD.

*Qianfoshan Rd. In the southern suburbs of Jinan. Tel: (0531) 6911792. Open: daily 7am–6pm. Admission charge.*

Silt gives the Yellow River its colour and makes it difficult to navigate

Heavenly guards and demon warriors at the Longmen Grottoes

## LANZHOU

The capital of Gansu province, in northern central China, lies along the old Silk Route on the upper Yellow River, near the Great Wall, in a region of mountains and deserts that has mostly been off the beaten track of Chinese civilisation. Lanzhou is a staging post for rail journeys to the north and west, with a connection to Urumqi (in the vast and sparsely populated Xinjiang Autonomous Region), and onward to Mongolia and Kazakhstan. It stands at an altitude of 1,600m.

### Five Springs Park
### (Wuquan Gongyuan)

The park stands at the foot of 2,000-m high Lanshan Mountain (Lanshan), the

summit of which can be reached by a 20-minute cable-car ride. The park itself is dotted with temples and waterfalls, and retains a sense of wild drama despite the man-made elements.
*Jiuquan Rd. South of the railway line. Open: daily 6.30am–10pm. Admission charge.*

### Gansu Provincial Museum
### (Gansu Sheng Bowuguan)

A silver-chased plate depicting the Greek god Bacchus, dating from the 2nd century BC, provides some evidence of the kind of goods that moved in an eastward direction along the Silk Road. The museum's exhibits are otherwise firmly Chinese, including a vast display of Neolithic pottery, and the famous

Galloping Horse of Gansu, flying with a swallow, dating from the Eastern Han period (AD 25–220), that was found in a nearby tomb.
*Xijin Xi Rd. Near the West Railway Station. Tel: (0930) 232 5049.*
*Open: Tue–Sun 9–11am & 2–5pm.*
*Closed: Mon. Admission charge.*

## White Pagoda Hill (Baita Shan)
The pagoda on the hill dates from the 14th-century Yuan dynasty, but has been restored several times. It is octagonal, has seven storeys, and is 17m high. The hill is a forested park, with other pavilions and temples.
*North bank of the river, near the Zhongshan Bridge. Open: daily 6.30am–10pm. Admission charge.*

## LUOYANG AND ENVIRONS
This city of one million inhabitants lies 30km south of the Yellow River in Henan province. Founded around 1200 BC, it was intermittently the capital of China from the Eastern Zhou dynasty (770 BC) until the Later Tang (AD 936). It is sometimes considered the eastern terminus of the Silk Route (*see p139*).

## Longmen Grottoes (Longmen Shiku)
Undoubtedly the most spectacular sight in the vicinity of Luoyang are the Buddhist cave carvings at Longmen. Altogether in this vast 'sculpture park' of 1,352 grottoes, there are more than 100,000 Buddha images, ranging in height from a few centimetres to 18m. The earliest date from AD 494, when they were begun under the orders of the Northern Wei-dynasty Emperor Hsaio Wen. The main sculptural groups are in the Binyang Caves (Binyang Dong) and the Ten Thousand Buddha Cave (Wanfo Dong). The latter specialises in musical and dancing imagery of the Buddha and his retainers.
*Located 20km south of Luoyang, along the Yi River, stretching for about 1km. Tel: (0379) 595 7645. Open: daily 8am–6pm. Admission charge.*

## Luoyang Municipal Museum (Luoyang Bowuguan)
The museum contains many relics from Luoyang's days of glory, including historical maps of the city, and artefacts recovered from tombs, such as sculpted horses and camels.
*Zhongzhou Rd. Adjacent to Wangcheng Park (Wangcheng Gongyuan). Tel: (0379) 393 7107. Open: Tue–Sun 10am–4pm. Closed: Mon. Admission charge.*

## White Horse Temple (Baima Si)
The Buddhist temple founded here in AD 68 was the first Buddhist temple in China. It has been rebuilt numerous times since the days when two monks arrived from India on white horses, bringing with them the *sutras* (ancient religious and philosophical texts) which they translated into Chinese. All the temple structures are recreations, mostly from the Ming era, and they include the hall where the original *sutras* are kept in a drawer.

The gateways are flanked by statues of the horses that carried the monks from India, whilst the monks themselves are buried in the walls.
*Located 10km east of Luoyang.*
*Open: daily 8am–6pm.*
*Admission charge.*

# Kunming and Environs

The 'city of eternal spring' is the description that the Yunnan provincial capital has gained, thanks to its location in the tropical south, near the borders with Vietnam, Laos and Myanmar. The potentially humid climate is modified by the fact that Kunming is situated at an altitude of 1,900m. Its metropolitan population of 1.3 million lives on the northern shore of Lake Dian (Dianchi), which is (at 330sq km) China's sixth-largest lake.

Celestial guardian of a temple in Kunming

Most of China's minority nationalities (*see p92*) live in Yunnan Province. Kunming, besides being an ideal base for exploring minority villages, is an attractive city. You could just stroll around and eat from stalls in its street markets. Most of its tourist sights are in the surrounding countryside.

## Bamboo Temple (Qiongzhu Si)

The Buddhist temple complex contains a marvellous set of 500 sculpted Buddhas dating from the 1880s, each with a different expression and engaged in some different activity.
*Located 12km northwest of Kunming. Open: daily 8am–6pm. Admission charge.*

## Black Dragon Pool (Heilong Tan)

A cluster of Taoist pavilions stands amidst the gardens that line up beside this pool, filled from a natural spring in the hills north of Kunming. The nearby Botanical Gardens, although far from extensive, allow for some walks through a wooded area, with clumps of camellias, azaleas, and rhododendrons among the other plants and shrubs.

*Located 11km north of Kunming. Tel: (0871) 515 0395. Open: daily 8am–5pm. Admission charge.*

## Golden Temple (Jindian)

This renowned Taoist temple sits in a scenic location on a forested hill. The present building dates from the Ming dynasty. In 1695, General Wu Sangui was sent by the new Manchu rulers to pacify the area, but Wu turned against his masters in Beijing. The Golden Temple became one of his palaces. Made of copper rather than gold, the 6.5-m high temple is estimated to weigh 300 tonnes.
*Located 7km northeast of Kunming. Tel: (0871) 515 4306. Open: daily 8am–5pm. Admission charge.*

## Green Lake Park (Cuihu Gongyuan)

As its name implies, this is a lake-dotted expanse of greenery, north of the city centre. Kunming is a busy, traffic-congested city that gets hot in summer, and the park is a much-needed, convenient place of escape.

*Located northwest of the city centre. Cuihu Rd. Open: daily 7am–8pm. Admission charge.*

## Lake Dian (Dianchi)

The lake begins in Kunming's southern suburbs and stretches for some 40km south of the city. Its western shores are rugged and overlooked by parks and temple complexes, while to the east are low-lying villages, fish farms, and fresh green rice paddy fields.

*Located at the foot of the Western Hills. Admission charge.*

## Stone Forest (Shilin)

Many visitors travel to Kunming for no other reason than to visit the limestone rocks of this so-called forest, 120km southeast of the city. The rocks have been eroded into fantastical shapes by wind and rain. Pathways have been constructed to make things easier, but one can easily get lost in the maze of paths and miss much worth seeing without a guide. Local Sani minority women, dressed in traditional costume, act as tour guides and point out the most interesting formations, such as the Lion Pavilion, Rhinoceros Gazing at the Moon, Mother and Son Travelling Together, and the Lotus Peak.

*Beyond Lunan Village. Open: daily 9am–6pm. Admission charge. Numerous minibus tours leave from Kunming city centre, departing as soon as they are full.*

The so-called Stone Forest is formed from eroded limestone rocks

China's minority peoples cling to their traditional way of life

## Western Hills (Xi Shan)

Also known as the Sleeping Beauty Hills, because they are supposed to resemble a reclining woman, these hills enclose a row of monumental buildings reached by a pathway overlooking Lake Dian.
*Western shore of Lake Dian, 15km south of Kunming.*
*Tel: (0871) 818 2211.*
*Open: daily 9am–6pm.*
*Admission charge.*

## Yuantong Temple (Yuantong Si)

This Tang dynasty Buddhist temple has been rebuilt many times since its foundation in the 10th century. Yuantong's pavilions include a white-jade statue of the Buddha. The principal pavilion is

octagonal, and is surrounded by a pool crossed by walkways and bridges, and dotted with plant-bedecked 'islets'.
*Yuantong St. Located just south of Kunming Zoo.*
*Open: daily 8am–6pm.*
*Admission charge.*

## Yunnan Ethnic Group Village

Capitalising on Kunming's status as a centre of minority peoples, this village features folk dancing and traditional music, and festivities and recreations of everyday life peculiar to the region. In addition, there are craft shops where local products are on sale.
*Dianchi Rd.*
*Tel: (0871) 316 3694.*

## MINORITIES

China's minorities represent 55 of the country's 56 recognised nationalities. With a total of around 70 million people, the minorities add up to a substantial population, even if they appear to be no more than a drop in the ocean of 1.3 billion Chinese.

The largest minority is the Zhuang (numbering about 12 million), living in Yunnan, Guangxi and Guangdong provinces. Other important groups are: the Yi of southern China; the Miao, whose 4 million people live across a huge swathe of southwestern China; Hainan Island's Li, whose fewer than 1 million people maintain a prickly cultural independence; the Uygur, the largest minority in the Xinjiang Uygur Autonomous Region; the Kazaks, famed for their horses; the Kirgiz, equally famed for their camels; and the Mongolians and Manchus in the north, descended from former conquerors of China (see pp20–21.)

## Yunnan Provincial Museum (Yunnansheng Bowuguan)

The most notable among a poor range of exhibits are those devoted to the costume and artefacts of the minority groups living in the province.

*2 Wuyi Rd. Corner of Dongfeng Xi Rd. Tel: (0871) 361 1548. Open: Mon–Sat 9.30am–4.30pm. Admission charge.*

## KUNMING AND THE SOUTH

As the gateway to the south of China, Kunming is the starting point for trips to the border area near Vietnam, Laos and Myanmar, which is slowly opening up to tourism.

## Dali and Xiaguan

Some 400km west of Kunming, these towns lie beside the scenic Erhai Lake (Erhai Hu), which has lakeside temples, and is crossed at various points by ferry boats. Both towns are minority centres.

## Jinghong

The centre of the Dai minority, Jinghong lies on the Mekong River (here known as the Lancang River) close to the Vietnamese border.

## Nanning

More easily reached by train from Guilin, Nanning, the capital of the Guangxi Autonomous Region, is a centre of the Zhuang, Miao, Yao, and Dong minority peoples. It contains research, educational, exhibition, and performance facilities. The Zuo River Scenic Area, southwest of Nanning, has karst scenery (limestone peaks) similar to that around Guilin, and boat trips leave from Nanning.

In Yunnan province a villager dries corn in front of his house

# Nanjing

Founded in 900 BC, the capital of Jiangsu province has endured a chequered history. It has been the capital of China several times and, for some months in 1912, it was the capital of Sun Yatsen's provisional government, following the overthrow of the Beijing-based Qing dynasty.

Emperor Hongwu protects his tomb

By any standards, Nanjing is a beautiful city, its tree-lined streets boasting a quarter of a million maple trees and a glorious display of chrysanthemums in autumn. The streets are busy, and the air no doubt is as polluted as anywhere else in China, but it seems less so, thanks to the breezes that sweep along the Yangtze River and down from the surrounding hills. Those hills, especially the Purple and Gold Mountains, are an additional attraction, and their cool air and open spaces make for a fine day out from the city.

## Chaotian Palace (Chaotian Gong)

The Worshipping Heaven Palace was originally a Ming-dynasty school for the children of high officials, later extended by the addition of a Confucian Temple in 1866. Together with other pavilions on the site, such as the Flying Cloud Pavilion and the Imperial Stele Pavilion, they form one of the most perfect monumental ensembles in China. Qing-dynasty emperors came to the temple to pay their respects to the sage.
*Mochou Rd. Several blocks east of Mochou Park. Tel: (025) 664 1983. Open: daily 9am–5pm. Admission charge.*

## Confucius Temple (Kong Fuzi Si)

In the atmospheric Fuzimiao district, where shopping, eating, and amusements abound, the temple is a symbol of a bygone age. Yet it remains popular with local Chinese, and rightly so. Recently rebuilt, it recreates the atmosphere of its Ming- and Qing-dynasty heritage, when its role changed from that of imperial educational establishment to temple. Outside the gate is a canal and a photogenic group of waterside houses.
*Gongyuan Rd. Off Zhonghua Rd. Tel: (025) 662 8639. Open: daily 8am–9pm. Admission charge.*

## Drum Tower (Gulou)

Dating from 1382, the tower displays a 2-m diameter drum that was beaten at night to sound the changes of the watch, and an inscribed stone stele mounted on an elephant.
*Beijing Xi Rd. At the traffic circle at the intersection with Zhongshan Bei Rd. Tel: (025) 663 3890. Open: daily 9am–5pm. Admission charge.*

## Linggu Temple (Linggu Si)

Part of the extensive monumental zone beneath the Purple Mountain, this temple was dedicated to Xuan Zang, one of the monks who brought the Buddhist scriptures to China from India. Next to it is the 60-m high Linggu Pagoda (Linggu Ta), which was designed in 1929 by the American architect, Henry Killam Murphy.

*Linggu Rd. East of the Sun Yatsen Mausoleum. Tel: (025) 446 111. Open: daily 7.30am–5.30pm. Admission charge.*

### Ming City Wall

Extensive sections remain of what was once an astonishing 33-km circumference defensive wall. Built by 200,000 labourers between 1366 and 1386, the wall averages a height of 12m and a width of 7m. Some of its 13 gates also survive, including Zhonghua Gate (Zhonghuamen) in the south, which has been restored and opened as a museum.

Sections of wall can be seen beside Xuanwu Lake, in the northwest close to the Yangtze River, and particularly in the south, beside the Qinhuai River.

### Ming Palace (Ming Gugong)

Little remains of the great palace on which the Forbidden City in Beijing is said to have been modelled. It was destroyed in various waves of rebellion and invasion, and only fragments of it survive today.

*Zhongshan Dong Rd. Junction of Yudao Street, west of Zhongshan Gate. Open: daily 10am–4pm. Admission charge.*

An incense burner in front of the entrance to a temple at Nanjing

Sun's Ming-style mausoleum is as splendid as any imperial palace

## Nanjing Museum (Nanjing Bowuguan)

Despite its name, this is the Jiangsu provincial museum, and features an extensive collection of objects from the Stone Age to 1919, including archaeological finds, porcelain, and antique astronomical instruments.
*4 Chaotiangong. Adjacent to Zhongshan Gate.
Tel: (025) 4465 317. Open: Tue–Sun 9am–5pm. Closed: Mon. Admission charge.*

## Purple and Gold Mountains (Zijinshan)

Overlooking the city, the Purple and Gold Mountains add to Nanjing's green reputation. At the foot of the mountains is the monumental zone that includes the Sun Yatsen Mausoleum and the

Linggu Temple. Walking is the best way to reach the summit, but there is also a cable car. Halfway up the pathway, you pass the Purple and Gold Mountain Observatory, which is linked to China's space programme.
*Northeastern edge of the city, beyond Xuanwu Lake.*

## Sun Yatsen Mausoleum (Zhongshan Ling)

Ironically, this is one of the most spectacular monuments in China – ironically, because the revolutionary Dr Sun Yatsen (*see box*) was a modest man and a democrat, who would surely be appalled to occupy a tomb so grandiose that even an emperor might have blushed at the sight. Nevertheless, the 8-

A doctor turned revolutionary, Sun Yatsen (1866–1925) aimed to heal the sickness of China under the weak Qing dynasty, when the country was prey to Western nations bent on conquest.

Born in Xiangshan, in Guangdong province, he spent most of his life outside China, being educated in Hawaii, then training as a doctor in Hong Kong, before practising medicine in Macao. In 1894, he founded the Society for the Revival of China, but had to flee the country after an unsuccessful uprising. Following the rebellion of the United League in 1911, Dr Sun was elected President of the Republic of China, but resigned after several months. Civil war ensued. In 1911, he founded the Kuomintang (Nationalist Party) and led it until his death. Dr Sun is widely revered for his Three People's Principles: nationalism, democracy, and people's livelihood.

hectare site is an impressive monument to the first President of the Republic of China. A series of pavilions and stairways ascends the slopes of the Purple and Gold Mountains, culminating in the mausoleum, built of dazzlingly white Fujian marble, surmounted by a blue-tiled roof, the whole recalling the Kuomintang (Nationalist) symbol of a white sun against a blue sky.

*Zhongshan Guangchang. On the southern slope of Purple Mountain. Tel: (025) 443 2799. Open: daily 8am–5pm. Admission charge.*

### Xuanwu Park (Xuanwu Gongyuan)

Apart from a series of connected islets and a thin strip around the shore, the park is basically all lake – but what a lake. Some 25km in circumference, all inside the city (and rich in carp), it can be toured by motorboat or barge. Children's amusement parks, a small zoo, pagodas, temples, and pavilions can be seen on the tour. The visitors are following an august tradition: Ming- and Qing-dynasty emperors used the lake for recreation.

*Northeast of the city centre, outside the city walls. There are several entrance gates, the main one being Xuanwu Gate off Zhongyang Rd. Tel: (025) 361 4286. Open: daily 8am–8pm. Admission charge.*

### Yangtze Bridge (Changjiang Daqiao)

See two giant bridges for the price of one. The 6.7km railway bridge is on the lower tier and above that is the 4.5km road bridge, crossing the great muddy expanse of the Yangtze. The Chinese are proud of having built these bridges in the 1960s (initially with Soviet aid), as the river had the reputation for being a 'natural moat that is hard to cross'.

*Northwest of the city, reached by Daqiao Nan Rd on the right bank and Daqiao Bei Rd on the left.*

Ancient instruments fascinate the visitor at the Purple and Gold Mountain Observatory

# Shanghai

The largest city in China, Shanghai is big, bustling, stylish, commercial, optimistic, and sure of itself. The politicos in Beijing may make the rules, but Shanghai's business-minded citizens are making the money.

Shanghai municipality covers 5,800sq km, of which 340sq km is occupied by the metropolitan district. Although located in the subtropical zone, it is close enough to the frigid north for average temperatures to drop to around 3°C in January.

**Imperialist Pawn**
Shanghai began life as a fishing village, and not until 1292 did it achieve any kind of independent status. From 1842 onwards, in the aftermath of the first Opium War, the British opened a 'concession' in Shanghai where drug dealers and other traders could operate undisturbed. French, Italians, Germans, Americans, and Japanese all followed. By the 1920s and 1930s, Shanghai was a boom town and an international byword for dissipation. The economy was built on the backs of cheap Chinese labour, while prostitution, crime, and opium addiction were rampant. When the Communists won power in 1949, they took a new broom to Shanghai, transforming the city into a model of the Revolution.

**Fast Track**
It is hard for infrastructure projects, however big, to keep pace with the city's growth. The recently completed ring

road has already become a traffic-jammed nightmare for motorists, and the newly developing subway system becomes overloaded almost as fast as new sections open. The constantly changing skyline of Pudong New Area now rivals that of Hong Kong as China's image of prosperity, with buildings such as the Pearl Oriental TV Tower and the Grand Hyatt – the highest hotel and bar in the world. Pudong radiates a feeling of space-age technology, in complete contrast to the conservative formality of the Bund directly opposite. The city lives on the fast track, yet occasionally takes time out to enjoy itself.

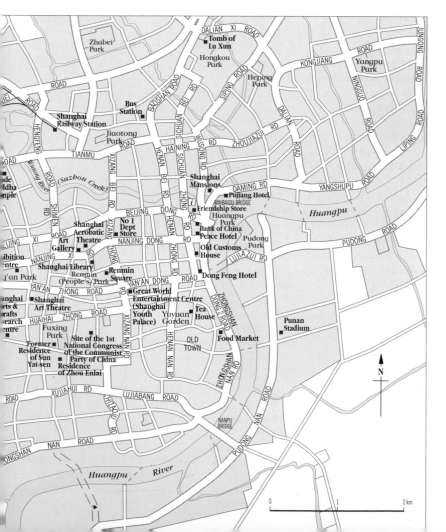

### The Bund (Waitan)

The Indian word for embankment was given by the British to this walkway beside the Huangpu River, bordered by 1920s and 1930s commercial buildings. Today, the Bund, a kind of elegant boardwalk, is a stylish place for Shanghainese to take the 'strongly scented' air of the river (which is somewhat fresher than that of the badly air-polluted city). Huangpu Park, at the northern end of the Bund, formerly the British-built Municipal Gardens, is where the notorious sign 'No Dogs and Chinese Allowed' was displayed in former times. Fortunately, the Chinese are not vengeful about this, and the park is also open to foreigners (daily from 5am to 10pm).
*From Suzhou Creek, at Huangpu Park, along the riverside to Yan'an Rd.*

### Hongkou Park (Hongkou Gongyuan)

A fair trek out along Sichuan Bei Road from the city centre leads eventually to this park, Shanghai's biggest, and a good place to observe people doing *tai chi* exercises in the morning. The park has an elongated lake at its heart, with islets, bridges, gardens, and pavilions. On its northern shore is a waterfall. In addition, there are two important monuments to the noted Chinese writer, Lu Xun (*see opposite*).
*Jiangwan Rd. Northern suburbs. Open: daily 8am–7pm. Admission charge.*

### Jade Buddha Temple (Yufo Si)

Built in 1882, on the southern edge of the city, the temple was moved, lock, stock, and jade Buddha statues, to its present location in 1918. Despite its relatively recent provenance, the temple complex has all the atmosphere of more ancient places, with followers of the Buddha praying before his statue, wreathed in incense smoke. The Jade Buddha on the second floor of the main pavilion is 1.9m high. Carved from a single piece of white jade, it was transported to China from Burma in 1882. A recently established Buddhist academy at the temple, which has a second white-jade Buddha statue, is a sign of the relative

### HUANGPU RIVER TRIP

The Huangpu River is a fascinating, but also disgracefully polluted, sight. Merchant ships, barges, ferry boats, cruise boats, junks, and private craft abound, along with an occasional warship of the Chinese navy, forcing its way into the waterway in an always-changing panorama.

Shanghai can also be viewed from the relative vantage point of the river, as well as of the huge and fast-developing Pudong New Area on the left bank. Cruise boats leave from the dock on the Bund near Huangpu Park (*tel: (021) 6374 4461*) for a 3- to 4-hour round trip to the junction with the Yangtze River.

tolerance with which the government now views religious practices.
*Anyuan Rd. Puto district in the northwest. Open: daily 8am–noon & 1–5pm. Admission charge.*

## Longhua Temple and Pagoda (Longhua Si and Longhua Ta)

Dating from AD 247, and built by the Emperor Sun Quan in honour of his mother, the 60m, seven-storey tower was rebuilt in 977, and is considered the finest ancient monument in Shanghai. Longhua Temple has pavilions, a bell tower, and a drum tower.
*Longhua Rd. Southern suburbs. Tel: (021) 6439 9399. Open: daily 9am–6pm. Admission charge.*

## Lu Xun Museum and Lu Xun Tomb (Lu Xun Bowuguan and Lu Xun Ling)

Lu Xun (1881–1936) was a writer who employed his literary skills in the effort to transform China from its imperial dynastic past to a modern, democratic future. The museum is only moderately interesting to non-specialists. The calligraphic inscription identifying Lu Xun's Tomb was designed by Chairman Mao Zedong.
*Hongkou Park. Tel: (021) 6540 2288. Museum open: Mon, Wed, Fri, & Sat 8.30–11.30am & Mon–Sat 1–4pm. Closed: Sun.*
*Tomb open: daily 8am–7pm. Admission charge.*

The Bund, Shanghai's riverside embankment lined with 1930s towers

The Huxingting Teahouse offers lake views in the Mandarin Gardens

## Mandarin Gardens and Bazaar (Yuyuan Shangchang)

These are also known as the Yu Gardens and Bazaar; the two parts are separate.

The Mandarin Gardens, dating from 1577, stand elegant in comparison with those of Suzhou (*see p108*), even though they are about as busy as any of the city streets. A mosaic of pools and pavilions – such as the Three Ears of Corn Hall (Sansui) and the Indicating Spring Hall (Dianchun) – plus rock gardens, plants, and bridges, this ought to be as restful as its wealthy creators intended, but it isn't.

The Chinatown-style Bazaar has no such pretensions: shoppers have to accept crowds. The mid-lake pavilion is the Huxingting Teahouse, reached by a 'zigzag' bridge – a defence against evil spirits, who can only move in a straight line.

*Yuyuan Rd. Between riverside Zhongshan Dong Rd & Henan Rd. Tel: (021) 6328 3251. Open: daily 8.30am–4.30pm. Admission charge.*

## Nanjing Dong Road (Nanjing Lu)

The city's – and perhaps all China's – busiest, most stylish, and most expensive shopping street runs west for 5km from the Bund to Yan'an Road. More than 300 shops and department stores do business on the street itself, along with restaurants, hotels, and cafés, and there are many more of all these on the adjacent side streets. The best point of departure is westwards from the Peace Hotel, at the junction of Nanjing Road and Zhongshan Dong Road.

## Renmin Square (Renmin Guangchang)

Like Beijing's Tiananmen Square – but less stiffly formal – Shanghai's main square is a vast ceremonial area. Laid out in 1951, it was designed for the great Communist parades. Nowadays, people prefer to fly kites and stroll.
*Off Xizang Zhong Rd, in the city centre.*

## Shanghai Botanical Gardens (Shanghai Zhiwuyuan)

This has a fine collection of around 9,000 potted flowers and trees, and specialises in the miniature representations of nature that are the hallmarks of a Chinese garden.
*Longhua Rd. Southern suburbs.*
*Tel: (021) 6451 3369.*
*Open: Mon–Sat 8am–5.30pm.*
*Closed: Sun. Admission charge.*

## Shanghai Museum (Shanghai Bowuguan)

Having moved to a new permanent location on Renmin Square, the museum has a superb venue for its outstanding collection of historical artefacts and dioramas. These date from prehistoric times onwards, and include bronze implements and ornaments, a wide-ranging porcelain collection, paintings, calligraphy, costumes, and tomb relics (including one featuring the skeletons of slaves killed to serve as retainers to their

dead master in the afterlife).
*Renmin Guanchang. Renmin Square.*
*Tel: (021) 6372 3500. Open: daily*
*9am–4pm. Admission charge.*

## Shanghai Zoo (Shanghai Dongwuyuan)

Unlike most zoos in China, Shanghai's is not necessarily a depressing experience, because the 280 different species of animals have more space to roam.
*Hongqiao Rd. Western suburbs, near*
*Shanghai Airport. Tel: (021) 6268 7775.*
*Open: Wed–Mon 7am–5pm.*
*Closed: Tue. Admission charge.*

## Site of the First National Congress of the Communist Party of China (Zhonggong Yidahuizhi)

This is the house where the Communist Party of China was inaugurated in a clandestine meeting within the French Concession area in July 1921, with Mao Zedong one of the 12 delegates.
*374 Huangpi Nan Rd.*
*Tel: (021) 5383 2171. Open: daily*
*9am–5pm; no admission after 4pm.*
*Admission charge.*

## Sun Yatsen's Residence (Sun Zhongshan Guju)

The father of the Chinese republic (*see p96*) lived here from 1920 to 1924, in a house bought for him by Chinese Canadians. It is still furnished in 1920s style, and displays various mementoes of Dr Sun, including photographs and his medical case.
*Xiangshan Rd. Near Fuxing Park.*
*Tel: (021) 6437 2954.*
*Open: Mon–Sat 9am–4.30pm.*
*Closed: Sun. Admission charge.*

# Walk: The Bund and Nanjing Road

This walk covers the old colonial-era heart of Shanghai, which stretches along the Huangpu River to form one of the world's most stylish riverside walkways, now the focal point of an increasingly affluent Shanghai.

*Allow 3 hours.*

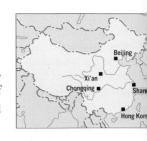

*Begin at Shanghai Mansions, on the northern bank of the Suzhou Creek.*

## 1 Shanghai Mansions

An Art Deco façade graces this elegant hotel, which overlooks the Suzhou Creek, Zhongshan Dong Lu (Zhongshan Dong Road), and the adjacent Bund. Suzhou Creek sounds romantic, but is a narrow, polluted mess of dirty water.
*Cross Waibaidu Bridge over the Suzhou Creek to Huangpu Park.*

## 2 Huangpu Park

This pretty little riverside park, formerly the British Municipal Gardens, once 'boasted' a notorious sign denying access to dogs and Chinese (*see p100*).
*Climb the steps on to the Bund, the riverside walkway. Huangpu River tour boats leave from a wharf near this point.*

## 3 The Bund

The colourful, swirling mass of people, all strolling along the paved walkway

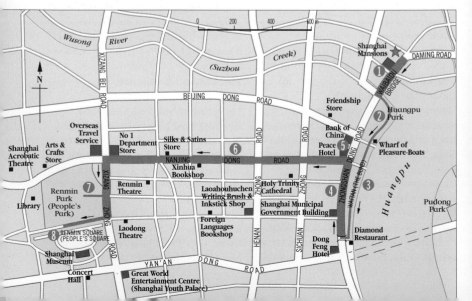

alongside the Huangpu River, is one of China's most appealing sights, with an air of energy and well-being.

Across the river is the tall, needle-pointed mast of the Television Tower, and the recently built 88-storey Jin Mao Building that dominates the vibrant Pudong New Area.

In the other direction, across busy Zhongshan Donglu, is the long row of solid-looking, 1920s- and '30s-vintage, former headquarters of the foreign banks and trading companies that once controlled Shanghai. These symbols of capitalism have been put to similar uses by the People's Republic, with the Bank of China at No. 22, and the red-fringed Shanghai Municipal Government building at No. 12 being among the most notable.

*Cross the footbridge over Zhongshan Dong Rd at the Diamond Restaurant and go north on Zhongshan Dong Rd.*

## 4 Zhongshan Dong Road

This gives an opportunity for closer inspection of the old commercial buildings facing the river, although the overall view is better from the Bund. Close up, the architectural details are more distinct, but the effect is diminished with the realisation that these buildings are no more notable than similar structures in Western cities.
*Turn left at the Peace Hotel into Nanjing Dong Rd.*

## 5 Peace Hotel

The Peace Hotel, formerly the Cathay Hotel, was one of the symbols of decadent old Shanghai, and still tries to retain at least a flavour of the raffish air

that surrounded it when Noël Coward wrote *Private Lives* here.
*Continue on Nanjing Dong Rd.*

## 6 Nanjing Dong Road (Nanjing Lu)

Nanjing Dong Road is one of the symbols of modern Shanghai, for here the ideology of making money dominates.

There is a frenetic air as shoppers move along the pavement and into the well-stocked shops and department stores. Anything that would be available in a Western shopping mecca is available on Nanjing Lu, from designer-label clothing and shoes, to high-tech consumer goods, to foods and stack-'em-high budget wares.
*Turn left at Shanghai No. 1 Department Store into Xizang Zhong Rd.*

## 7 Renmin Park (Renmin Gongyuan)

A welcome break from the relentlessly urban and polluted streets, Renmin Park's ponds and grassy spaces are popular with the Shanghainese, who can be seen doing their pre-work *tai chi* exercises here in the early morning. In the good old bad old days, this was the Shanghai Racecourse.
*Continue on Xizang Zhong Rd to Renmin Square.*

## 8 Renmin Square (Renmin Guangchang)

Typical of the new urban landscape, this vast and soulless expanse of concrete, Renmin (or People's) Square, at least provides space to stretch one's legs and breathe air not directly polluted by fuming exhaust pipes. The sparklingly modern Municipal Museum stands on its southern axis.

Outside the walls of a Chinese garden may be some of the noisiest and most polluted streets on earth. Inside, the peace that reigns has inspired poets and painters over centuries, and still has the power to help visitors unwind from a stressful day, while breathing the scented air of tranquillity. Gardens are one of the most precious legacies of China's 5,000-year-old civilisation, and they continue to delight the senses.

A Chinese garden is much more than nature in miniature; it represents the essence of nature. The first recorded Chinese botanical garden was established at Changan (Xi'an) in 111 BC, although China's devotion to flowers, as indicated by poetry and

painting, reaches back thousands of years earlier. A common name for China is 'the Flowery Land'. Yet flowers are not the principal element in a Chinese garden. Pools, goldfish, trees, rocks, and white walls (symbolising mist) provide more than a setting for floral displays. They bring the vastness and changeability of the natural world down to a human scale, a truly fit place for meditation.

Change is characteristic of nature, so observing change is an integral part of

The natural world reduced to human scale: ancient gardens in Shanghai and Suzhou

the inspiration and design of a garden. Pavilions are laid out so that different aspects of the garden can be observed as the seasons unfold. Peonies are the stars of spring; pools laden with water-lilies the highlight of summer; in autumn, chrysanthemums and orchids take centre stage; the stark effects of bare rock and chill winds add inspiration to winter afternoons in heated pavilions. Wide vistas alternate with constricted views, adding to the contrasting effects that are being sought.

Most Chinese cities have at least one garden that is worth visiting. Among the more beautiful are **Shanghai's Yuyuan (Yu Garden)** and those in and around the west lake of **Hangzhou city**, but the finest are to be found in **Suzhou** (see p108) and **Beijing** (see p43). Most city tourist maps list the gardens to be seen.

# Suzhou and Environs

Suzhou, the city of canals and gardens, 85km west of Shanghai, was called the 'Venice of the East' by Marco Polo. An ancient Chinese proverb states: 'In Heaven there is Paradise; on Earth there is Suzhou'. The city's love affair with gardens dates back 2,500 years and continues still. At the time of the Ming dynasty (1368–1644) there were 250 gardens, of which about a hundred survive, although only a few are open to the public. Tourists can pause in contemplation, experiencing nature as the poets, painters, and philosophers did, but be sure to arrive before the crowds, who strip the gardens of their calm.

One of Suzhou's evocative gardens

## Blue Wave Pavilion (Canglangting)

Reached by bridge across a brook, the one-hectare Blue Wave Pavilion is the only garden not completely enclosed by a wall. In addition, it is the oldest garden in Suzhou, with a wilder design than the others, with rockeries and artificial hillocks decorated with clumps of bamboo. It takes its name from a waterside pavilion built in 1044 by the poet Su Shunqin.
*Renmin Rd. Between the Nanlin Hotel and the long distance bus station. Open: daily 8am–5pm, 4.30pm in winter. Admission charge.*

## Humble Administrator's Garden (Zhuozheng Yuan)

The original garden was gambled away by the son of the 'humble administrator', a former official who laid it out in 1522. The superb ensemble is some 5 hectares in extent, and one of the finest gardens in China. Water is the main theme here, with the extensive pools overlooked by pavilion-studded banks and dotted with islets reached by graceful bridges or narrow stone causeways.
*Dongbei St. Northeast corner of the old city. Tel: (0512) 753 9869. Open: daily 8am–5pm, 4.30pm in winter. Admission charge.*

## Garden for Lingering In (Liu Yuan)

Plants, trees, and rocks abound in this 3-hectare garden, including a 6.5-m high rock which dominates its surroundings. The pavilions are also impressive, including the finely furnished Hall of Mandarin Ducks and the Hall of Trees and Springs, beside the Pool for Watching Clouds. The principal beauty spots are connected by a 700m corridor. Hundreds of windows latticed in differing floral patterns look out on the rocks, plants, and water, giving the effect of pictures at an exhibition viewed through constantly changing frames.
*Liuyuan Rd. Northwestern suburbs, beyond the moat. Tel: (0512) 533 7940.*

*Open: daily 7.30am–5.30pm.*
*Admission charge.*

## Master of the Nets Garden (Wangshi Yuan)

At just half a hectare, this is the smallest of Suzhou's gardens, but it compensates with an elegant design that has been widely influential as a model for other Chinese gardens. Courtyards, corridors, and pavilions give observation points, and names like the Pine Viewing and Painting Appreciating Hall and the Moon and Wind Pavilion, convey the flavour of the contemplative hours spent here by the wealthy and leisured former owners. On summer evenings, the garden remains open beyond its normal closing time, and is illuminated with lanterns, while musicians and folk dancers entertain visitors.
*Shiquan St. Southeastern corner of the old city, between the Nanling and Suzhou hotels. Open: daily 8am–3.30pm.*
*Admission charge.*

## North Temple Pagoda (Beisi Ta)

Nine storeys and 76m high, the octagonal pagoda dates from the late-10th century, though it has been rebuilt several times. The view from the top is superb and well worth the exertion.
*Renmin Rd. Northern sector of the old city. Open: daily 8am–5.30pm.*
*Admission charge.*

Suzhou is one of many contendors for the title 'Venice of the East'

## Suzhou Bazaar (Suzhou Shangchang)

The 'bazaar' is an attractive shopping and restaurant zone that stands on both sides of the main east-west city centre street (Guanqian Street), which is itself a pedestrian precinct.

## Suzhou Silk Museum (Suzhou Bowuguan)

Though fairly small, this informative museum covers Suzhou's history and culture. Exhibits of silk recall the importance of the centuries-old industry to the region.

*Renmin Rd, Dongbei St. Near the Humble Administrator's Garden. Open: daily 9am–5pm. Admission charge.*

## Temple of Mystery (Xuanmiaoguan)

Considered to be among the finest Taoist temples in China, the Temple of Mystery dates originally from AD 279, although it was destroyed in 1860 and rebuilt some years later. The great Sanqing Hall, at the heart of the temple, is supported by 60 pillars and topped by a double roof.

*Guanqian St. In the central Suzhou Bazaar district. Open: daily 9am–6pm. Admission charge.*

## Tiger Hill (Huqiu)

So-named because a white tiger is said to have appeared here during the burial of Emperor He Lu in the 5th century BC. The spectacular Tiger Hill Pagoda has tilted dangerously, and has had to be braced to stop it from falling over.

*Northwest of Suzhou, 5km from the city. Open: daily 8am–6pm. Admission charge.*

## West Garden (Xi Yuan)

This is actually a Buddhist temple, with gardens attached, dating from the 16th century. Its most notable sight is a series of rooms filled with 500 representations of the Buddha, each with a different character and expression.

*Liuyuan Rd. Western suburbs, adjacent to the Lingering Garden.*
*Open: daily 8am–7pm, 5pm in winter. Admission charge.*

Musicians entertain at Tiger Hill

One of the most beautiful of cities, Suzhou is a tourist hot spot

# Tour: Suzhou

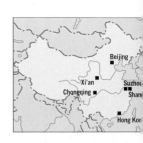

Few of China's increasingly industrialised and crowded cities are so pleasant to walk around as Suzhou, with its tree-fringed streets, houses built on a human scale, and generally mild climate – and its magnificent gardens are a treat fit for an emperor. Although small as Chinese cities go, Suzhou is still big enough that the distances may be too great for walking all the way. This tour through the city of gardens combines walking with taxi and pedicab rides, but if time and energy allow, you will do better just to walk.

*Allow a whole day; there is little point in making the tour unless you visit some of the gardens.*

*Begin at West Garden in the western suburbs.*

### 1 West Garden (Xi Yuan)

Built around a 16th-century Buddhist temple complex, rebuilt in 1892, the gardens feature a pavilion containing no fewer than 500 larger-than-lifesize Buddha images, each of which wears a different expression. A 1,000-arm Buddha guards the entrance.

*Cross Huqiu Rd to Liuyuan Rd and the entrance to the Lingering Garden.*

### 2 Garden for Lingering In (Liu Yuan)

You will probably want to linger in one of China's most glorious gardens, although not the biggest in Suzhou. Some 200 variously shaped windows look out on to the wooded, floral, and watery scene beyond (*see p108*).

*It is probably best to take a taxi through the Changmen Gate, along Xizhongshi St and Dongzhongshi St, then left on Renmin Rd to the North Temple Pagoda.*

### 3 North Temple Pagoda (Beisi Ta)

The top of the 9-storey North Temple Pagoda offers an unsurpassed view over the city. This is the largest pagoda south of the Yangtze River (*see p109*).

*Continue along Xibei St, to the Humble Administrator's Garden on Dongbei St.*

### 4 Humble Administrator's Garden (Zhuozheng Yuan)

Far from being humble, this extensive garden is formed by three connected gardens and adds up to an ideal image of the elements that form the traditional Chinese garden: water, rocks, bridges, pavilions, plants, and trees, blended into a restful harmony (*see p108*).

*Turn into Yuanlin Lu for the Lion Grove Garden.*

### 5 Lion Grove Garden (Shizilin Yuan)

So-named because many of its Lake Tai

rocks are shaped like lions in various poses, the garden has a stone boat 'anchored' in its large central lake.
*An alternative at this point is to rent a pedicab. Come out on to canal-lined Lindun Rd and turn right into Guanqian St, where you leave the pedicab.*

## 6 Suzhou Bazaar (Suzhou Shangchang)

A stroll through this pedestrianised area with shops and restaurants makes for a change of pace from the gardens (*see p110*).
*Turn left on to Renmin Rd for the Joyous Garden.*

## 7 Joyous Garden (Yi Yuan)

A century old, this is the newest of Suzhou's gardens, formed around a pool crossed by a crooked bridge.

*From here, either walk or go by pedicab along Renmin Rd to the Blue Wave Pavilion Garden.*

## 8 Blue Wave Pavilion Garden (Canglangting)

The Blue Wave is a wild little place, depending more for its effect on a rugged interpretation of nature than on mirrored pools of water (*see p108*).
*Retrace your steps along Renmin Rd to Shiquan St and continue to the Master of the Nets Garden, reached by a narrow side alley.*

## 9 Master of the Nets Garden (Wangshi Yuan)

This is an even smaller garden, alongside the residence of a retired official who preferred its tranquillity to the exercise of power (*see p109*).

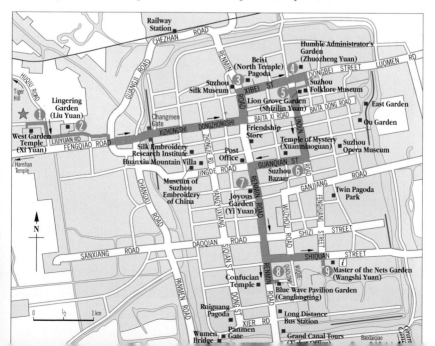

# Grand Canal

At 1,800km, the Grand Canal (Dayunhe) is the longest artificial waterway in the world. It stretches from Hangzhou to Beijing, passing through Suzhou and Wuxi on the way. The canal's average width is 30m. At present it is not possible to navigate the entire length, but this may change as China takes steps to re-open the canal fully for commerce and tourism.

Construction began in the 5th century BC to facilitate the transport of rice from the Yangtze Valley to Beijing. During succeeding centuries, rivers and lakes were linked by artificial stretches of waterway to create the whole. The Grand Canal was fully opened in the early 7th century AD and provided the main connection between north and south China.

Silting, combined with the growth of railways, saw the decline of the historic

waterway. It stayed in use in stretches, and on a smaller scale. In places, houses were built on what had been its bed.

Despite the advent of cruise tourism along the Hangzhou to Yangzhou stretch, this waterway has remained a muddy mess. Yet it traverses beautiful countryside and some lovely cities, offering a glimpse of how it must have been when imperial barges and grain boats plied its route.

Parts of the Grand Canal continue to be used some 1,500 years after it was constructed

# Wuxi and Environs

With a history that dates back 3,000 years, to the Shang and Zhou dynasties, Wuxi fell on hard times when the tin deposits that gave it life ran out – its name actually means 'no tin'. Although the Grand Canal runs right through it, and the town remains a centre of silk production, Wuxi itself is a smoky industrial centre; the main points of interest lie some 10km to its southwest, around the shores of Lake Taihu.

Li Garden, Wuxi

### Grand Canal (Dayunhe)

Few places are better situated for watching ordinary life on the Grand Canal than Wuxi. The city's prosperity was a direct result of its position on the canal, and barges still maintain a fairly small-scale traffic on the water, while old houses with wooden balconies are clustered together on the banks.
*There are numerous points of observation, thanks to the city's numerous bridges, the best being those on Renmin Xilu and Liangxi Lu.*

### Lake Taihu (Taihu)

At 2,235sq km, this is one of China's biggest lakes. Its best-known attribute may not be its fresh waters and the fish they produce, but the big limestone rocks, worn, holed, and shaped by the action of wind and water, which are an integral feature of the best Chinese gardens. Lake Taihu is a scenic spot of some grandeur, the extensive waters mirroring the hilly shores and dotted with fishing boats, fish farms, junks, pleasure cruisers, and islets. Some of the best points have been taken over by

tacky amusement parlours and other 'attractions' that cater to local visitors. An exception is the Orchid Conservation and Research Centre, which must be just about unique in China, if only because admission is free!

Most of these locations are on Turtle Head Isle (Yuantouzhu) – which is actually the tip of the Chongshan Peninsula – and they can be reached by a distinctly shaky monorail, while the rest of the isle is reached by tour boats from Wuxi, or by powerboat from various points along the shore. Tour boats leave from Turtle Head Isle for a short cruise to the Three Hills Isles (Sanshan), an island park that offers superb views across the lake.
*Southwest of Wuxi.*

### Li Garden (Liyuan)

Very nearly in Lake Taihu, the garden depends on water for its effect as much as on its trees, pavilions, and rockeries. The Lake-Gazing Pavilion looks out over the lake. Dating from 1930, the garden was expanded after 1949. A Stone Boat adds to the nautical flavour.

*Hubin Lu. Lakeside, east of the Baojie Bridge to Turtle Head Isle. Open: daily 6.30am–5.30pm. Admission charge.*

### Plum Garden (Meiyuan)

This suffers in comparison with the Li Garden because its pavilions are in a poor state of repair, but the ragged nature of the park may actually be refreshing after the over-manicured look of most Chinese gardens. Kingfishers dart around the main pool, and a visit early in the year will find the plum trees – symbols of beauty, elegance, and endurance – in blossom.

*Liangxi Lu. Near the Taihu Hotel. Open: daily 6.30am–5.30pm. Admission charge.*

### Xihui Park (Xihui Gongyuan)

This city park merges with the wide-open spaces of Hui Hill (Huishan) to provide an airy escape from Wuxi's smog. On Xi Hill (Xishan) stands the Ming-dynasty Dragon Light Pagoda (Longguang Ta), from whose top a fine view over the city and nearby Lake Taihu is in prospect.

*Hehui Lu. Across the Grand Canal from Renmin Lu. Open: daily 6am–8pm. Admission charge.*

Turtle Head Isle, Lake Taihu, is popular with artists and tourists

# Porcelain

In films, the vase that gets broken by a clumsy guest or a jilted lover is always a priceless piece of Ming – and the fact that it was old somehow does not mollify its owner. Chinese porcelain has a pedigree stretching back well before the Ming (AD 1368–1644) to the Song Dynasty (AD 960–1279) and earlier (it probably originated in the 6th century AD). It was unknown in Europe until around 1300, where the earliest imports were thought to be made of some semi-precious material and often set in gold or silver. Not until the early 18th century was its manufacture fully mastered in Europe, at the Meissen works in Germany.

A hard, thin, vitrified, and translucent ceramic, porcelain is made from special (feldspathic) clays, whose constituents vary from place to place. It is fired at high temperature, with the glaze being fused to the body. Even today, porcelain is a craft product highly prized by collectors. It is hand-glazed and fired in kilns whose temperature is determined by the skill of the master potter.

## The Blues

Blue-and-white porcelain, perfected in the Ming period, was the high point of Chinese porcelain design. The form took Europe by storm, and it continues to do so in such makes as Delft blue. The technique was a complicated one to perfect, and involved painting cobalt on to the clay body before covering it with glaze and firing. Lightness, translucency, and

delicacy were all achieved by the mid-15th century, and the vessels were highly prized by courts and wealthy individuals around the world.

The isolated town of Jingdezhen, on the Chang River in Jiangxi province, has long been the porcelain capital of China, thanks to its fine kaolin clay. A **Museum of Ceramic History** (Taoci Lishi Bolanqu) illuminates the story, and visits can be made to the town's many kilns where white-glazed, celadon, blue-and-white, overglaze colour, and other styles of porcelain are all produced.

### Collections

The **Shanghai Museum** in People's Square, Shanghai, and the **Beijing Art Museum** both have rare and exquisite exhibits. The **Tsui Museum of Art** in Hong Kong has a comprehensive collection that covers 5,000 years.

Modern reproductions of porcelain originals range from fine decorative vases to everyday objects such as soup bowls and spoons (left)

# Xi'an and Environs

The capital of Shaanxi province, in northern central China, Xi'an was the country's ancient capital, and has undergone a renaissance as a tourist centre, both for its own Tang, Han, and Ming dynasty monuments, and as a base for visiting the fabulous army of terracotta warriors to the city's east. During the Tang period, when the city was called Chang'an, it had two million inhabitants, and was the eastern terminus of the Silk Route (*see p139*).

An elegant pavilion at Huaqing Hot Springs

### Banpo Neolithic Village (Banpo Bowuguan)
The 6,500-year-old village is of interest to scholars of the Yangshao Culture, and also to tourists, because the layout of the museum allows visitors to walk among the remains of the villagers' huts. Several hundred graves have been uncovered. Weapons, tools, farming and fishing implements are on display.
*Banpo Rd. In the eastern suburbs, across the Chanhe River. Tel: (029) 353 2482. Open: daily 9am–5pm. Admission charge.*

### Bell Tower (Zhong Lou)
The tower where the bell was rung to signify the opening of the city gates, and which now offers a fine view of the busy city, dates from 1384. It incorporates an antique store with carved beams and a beautifully painted ceiling (*see p124*).
*Nanda St. In the centre of the old city. Tel: (029) 721 4665. Open: daily 8.30am–5pm. Admission charge.*

### Big Wild Goose Pagoda (Da Yan Ta)
This pagoda gained its curious name

from the legend that a nearby temple was built to honour a sacred goose. The pagoda dates from AD 652, but was recently rebuilt. Its seven storeys and 284 interior steps lead to a fine viewpoint (*see p125*).
*Yanta Rd. Southeastern suburbs, near the History Museum. Tel: (029) 525 3802. Open: daily 8.30am–6pm. Admission charge.*

### City Wall
The 14km-long city wall dates from the 14th century and is built on earlier Tang foundations. It has recently been restored and is an impressive 12-m high monument to the city's former importance. There are four great fortified gates: the North Gate (Beimen), South Gate (Nanmen), East Gate (Dongmen), and West Gate (Ximen).
*The walls are ringed by Huancheng Rd (itself divided into quarters called Bei, Nan, Dong, and Xi).*

### Drum Tower (Gulou)
Drums were beaten from here at night as the city gates were about to close.

Built in 1380, the tower is 34m high.
*Beiyuanmen. Between the Great Mosque
and the Bell Tower. Tel: (029) 727 4580.
Open: daily 8.30am–5pm.
Admission charge.*

## Great Mosque (Da Qingzhen Si)

Set amidst the rambling and jumbled
alleys of Xi'an's old Muslim quarter, the
mosque, founded in AD 742, is an
interesting example of how traditional
Islamic architectural and decorative
styles adapted to China – mostly being
dominated by the Chinese forms
(*see also p124*).
*Huajue Xiang. West of the Drum Tower
in the city centre's old Muslim quarter.
Tel: (029) 721 9807. Open: daily
8am–6pm. Admission charge.*

## Huaqing Hot Springs (Huaqing Chi)

This superb thermal springs complex
lies not far from the terracotta army site,
some 30km east of Xi'an. The pools,
bath-houses and garden pavilions are
being restored to their Tang-dynasty
glory, when this was a favoured resort
of emperors.

The famous 'Xi'an incident'
occurred here in 1936. At this historic
event, the nationalist leader, Chiang
Kaishek, was held a prisoner by his
generals until he agreed to form an
alliance with the Communists against
the invading Japanese.
*Lintong County. South of the Qin
Army Vaults. Open: daily 7am–5.30pm.
Admission charge.*

Xi'an's Bell Tower from where the dawn bell was rung every day

## Qin Terracotta Army Museum (Qin Bingmayong Bowuguan)

Many visitors will consider this the most fascinating sight in China. As recently as 1974, there was nothing here. That year some peasants digging a well chanced upon an awesome scene. They broke through an underground vault where they discovered 6,000 life-size figures of terracotta soldiers and horses in battle array, each face different – an eternal imperial guard for the founder of the Qin dynasty, the Emperor Qin Shihuangdi, whose tomb is nearby.

Two more vaults filled with terracotta warriors have since been uncovered and opened to the public, one of them a 'command post' for the buried legions. Archaeologists believe other such pits await discovery. Two teams of bronze chariots with horses and charioteer have also been discovered, and are displayed in a separate building.

The scene inside the vaults is charged with mystery, as visitors come face to face with the silent army. Unfortunately, they also come face to face with a far from silent army of fellow visitors, a shuffling queue that gives you little chance to stop and admire the sight (photography is also forbidden). However, there is not much the Chinese can do about the number of tourists eager to see the buried army, and they do their best to accommodate them.
*Lintong County. Located 40km northeast of Xi'an. Open: daily 8am–6pm. Admission charge.*

## Shaanxi Historical Museum (Shaanxi Lishi Bowuguan)

This superb new building is big enough – as it has to be – to do justice to the vast archaeological zone that much of Shaanxi seems to be, particularly the area around Xi'an (ancient Chang'an). A vast

The tomb of Emperor Qin Shihuangdi

The terracotta warriors: a formidable army, in full battle array, forming the imperial guard

range of objects from all periods is on display, and even the famous terracotta warriors are no more than an element in a long and fascinating story.
*Xiaozhai Rd. Near the Big Wild Goose Pagoda. Tel: (029) 520 4728. Open: daily 8am–6pm in summer, 8.30am–5.30pm in winter. Admission charge.*

## Small Wild Goose Pagoda (Xiao Yan Ta)

As its name implies, this is a smaller cousin to the Big Wild Goose Pagoda, having lost its top two storeys to an earthquake in the 16th century. Still 43m high, it is a graceful structure dating from the early 7th century, which may be climbed for its view (*see p125*).
*Youyi Xi Rd. South of Nanmen Gate. Tel: (029) 525 3455. Open: daily 8.30am–5pm. Admission charge.*

## Tomb of Qin Shihuangdi (Qin Shihuangdi Ling)

The Emperor Qin Shihuangdi, who ruled from 221 BC until his death in 209 BC, succeeded in uniting China, bringing the Warring States period to an end. Yet it is for his mausoleum and the nearby buried army of terracotta warriors (*see above*) that he is best known. The mausoleum's inner sanctuary is 2.5km in circumference, and the outer boundary stretches for 6km. Archaeologists have postponed its complete excavation and opening to the public, but it is possible to climb the 40-m high tumulus and ponder the life and times of the megalomaniac ruler buried beneath.
*Lintong County. Located 1.5km from the Qin Terracotta Army Museum. Open: daily 9am–5pm. Admission charge.*

# Tour: Xi'an City

A big and not especially attractive city, but with some superb monuments scattered around, Xi'an is probably best toured through a combination of walking, taxi, and pedicab.

*Allow 4 hours.*

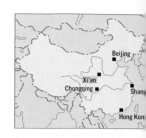

*Begin at the North Gate.*

## 1 North Gate (Beimen)

The city's powerful 14th-century Ming-dynasty wall, with its moats, towers, and gates is being restored, thus recreating some of the glory of Xi'an's past (*see p120*). Much earlier, as Chang'an, it had been the imperial capital of the Han and Tang dynasties. This gate is one of four set at the principal compass points.
*It is best to go by taxi along Beida St, then right into Lianhu Rd to Lianhu Park.*

## 2 Lianhu Park (Lianhu Gongyuan)

Parks are not numerous in Xi'an, although many avenues are lined with trees. This slight detour passes among the lakes and greenery before re-emerging on to the fuming streets.
*Come out on to Honghu St, Beiguangji St and right into Xiyang St to the Great Mosque and the small and animated alleyways around it.*

## 3 Great Mosque (Da Qingzhen Si)

After fighting your way past the souvenir stalls, you will find that the mosque (*see also p121*) is a relaxed and welcoming place, as well as an appropriately tranquil refuge from the outside world. A bewildering array of architectural styles almost belies its status as an Islamic shrine, but Xi'an's Muslim population attends religiously. The prayer hall, at the far end of the interior garden, is not accessible to non-Muslims.
*Continue on Xiyang St and turn right to the Drum Tower.*

## 4 Drum Tower (Gulou)

The Drum Tower stands at the heart of Xi'an's old Muslim quarter which is perhaps more interesting than the tower itself, with some marvellous little restaurants serving fiery spiced food. The tower was used to sound the curfew before the opening and closing of the city gates.
*Continue south of the Drum Tower and turn left on to Xida St to the Bell Tower.*

## 5 Bell Tower (Zhong Lou)

There is a notable view from this centrally located point. Equally notable is the carved ceiling and the fact that the 14th-century wooden tower hangs together without the help of nails (*see p120*).
*Come south into Nanda St and left into Dongmutoushi St for the Forest of Stone Stelae.*

## 6 Forest of Stone Stelae

This remarkable collection consists of ancient writings and calligraphy carved on thousands of stone tablets. The content is of most interest to scholars, but the setting, in an old Confucian temple, means that non-specialists can enjoy the sight.

*Take Shuyuanmen St west to the South Gate.*

## 7 South Gate (Nanmen)

This is another of the four principal gateways in the Ming-era walls, marking the boundary of the old city (*see p120*).

*It is probably best to go by taxi or pedicab to Youyi Xilu and the Small Wild Goose Pagoda.*

## 8 Small Wild Goose Pagoda (Xiao Yan Ta)

The 7th-century pagoda's 15 tiers gradually diminish in size as they ascend, above the grounds of the Jianfu Temple, to its summit (*see p123*).

*A taxi or pedicab is essential for the next leg, to the Big Wild Goose Pagoda.*

## 9 Big Wild Goose Pagoda (Da Yan Ta)

Dating originally from the 7th century, this is the best of the two pagodas to climb. At 64m, it is 21m higher than the Small Wild Goose Pagoda, and has a better view – though Xi'an's ordinary skyline may make this a questionable use of one's energy (*see p120*).

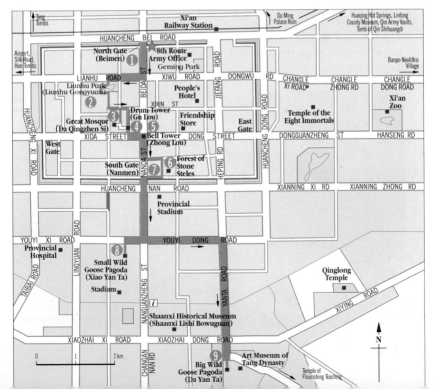

# Inventions

It seems ironic that so many of China's difficulties with colonial powers in the 19th century were caused by its inferior technology, because China has a proud record of innovation stretching back for centuries. Practical and widespread application of the products, however, was what was lacking.

Gunpowder, the world's oldest explosive, a mixture of sulphur, charcoal, and saltpetre, was in use in China as early as the 10th century during the Song dynasty, when it was used in grenades and rockets, and later in firearms. Another invention, which revolutionised warfare in its time, was the stirrup, which permitted greater power in the delivery of a lance blow.

## Peaceful Processes

Paper and blockprinting were more peaceable. Paper was in use by the 2nd century AD, and there are indications that it may have been invented as early as the 2nd century BC. The earliest known printed book (AD 868), using the woodblock method, is a Buddhist Diamond Sutra. Mechanical clocks, the wheelbarrow, suspension bridges, paddle-boats, canal locks, and piston bellows are all Chinese developments.

China gave the world kites, porcelain, the magnetic compass, and even a pre-vaccination form of immunisation against smallpox. Then there are noodles, and tea, whose cultivation and consumption began in China.

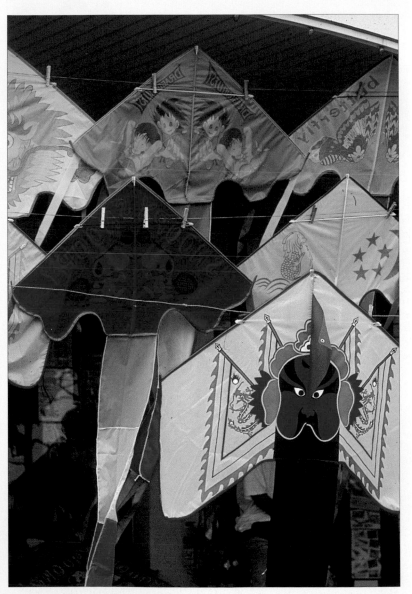

Tea, silk, and kites are all Chinese innovations

# Natural Beauty

No country that occupies such a vast extent of the planet as China could be short of places renowned for natural beauty. This seems even more true because of the great emphasis Chinese poets and painters have always placed on their land's scenic wonders, as though beauty, to delight the senses and inspire the mind, was part of the compact between the Middle Kingdom and the Heaven that watched over it.

Clear water and peaks that touch the clouds

The beauty is still there, although diminished by those familiar markers of the modern age – pollution, over-development, and exploitation for tourism. Appreciation of nature depends to an extent on having the leisure and

The pristine waters of Yangtze flow through Yunnan province

wealth to indulge it. The officials and intellectuals of the past had both, but it is a fair assumption that the peasants who laboured to maintain the privileges of the favoured few had a less favourable opinion of the harsh landscapes that form two-thirds of the country. Now, under the influence of a burgeoning economy and a more equitable distribution of wealth, ordinary Chinese can join foreign tourists in appreciating China's scenic wonders.

### Sacred Highs

Five Holy Mountains (Wu Yue) is the collective name for the five mountains that are regarded in Chinese legend as gathering places of the gods, now all places for religious pilgrimages and sightseeing trips.

**Hengshan**, the first of the five, is 310km south of Changsha (in Hunan province), and its 72 peaks have around 20 Taoist and Buddhist temples. Its namesake, **Hengshan**, lies 80km south of Datong (in Shaanxi province), and has the 1,400-year-old Hanging Monastery (Xuan Kongsi) clinging to its mountainous face. **Huashan** is 120km east of Xi'an (in Shaanxi) and its 2,200m summit is reached along a stairway that soars above sheer drops. **Songshan**, 60km southeast of Luoyang (in Henan), is the site of the Shaolin Temple, where martial arts are among the religious rites. **Taishan,** 50km south of Jinan (in Shandong), is the most famous and the most revered of the five mountains. Emperors climbed to its summit, as did Confucius and Mao Zedong. A sixth mountain, **Emeishan** (in Sichuan province), is at least an 'honorary member' of the club, while **Huangshan** (in Anhui province) is considered the most beautiful mountain in China.

### Wilder Side

There are many, much more impressive mountains. The Himalayas stand on the borders of Tibet and Nepal, while China proper has the Kunlun range, whose peaks reach 7,000m, and whose melting snows feed both the Yangtze and the Yellow rivers. In the remote Xinjiang Autonomous Region, in Qinghai and Inner Mongolia, are some of the most remarkable natural formations on earth. These include the Gobi and Taklamakan deserts, the Qinghai, China's largest saltwater lake, and the scorchingly hot Turpan (Turfan) Depression.

### Sea and Sand

Along its 18,000km coastline, China has an abundance of beaches and rugged shores, yet somehow China does not conjure up a vision of the ideal seaside holiday. This is partly because the coastal zone is heavily populated and industrialised, and the quality of the seawater is uncertain, to say the least. Even so, a beach holiday infrastructure of international quality is fast developing on the subtropical island of Hainan in the south.

The Singing Sand Dunes of Dunhuang, near the Turpan Depression

# Wildlife

China's wildlife has a hard time. Anything that flies, swims, walks, crawls, or slithers is fair game for the cooking pot, and with more than a billion human mouths to feed, much natural habitat has been converted to agricultural use. The exploitative attitude to wildlife has spilled over into other areas. Few Westerners will feel comfortable in Chinese zoos, where animals have little space and are often tormented by visitors.

Fortunately, this is not the whole story. Large areas of China consist of wilderness or semi-wilderness unsuited to agriculture, where the wildlife, adapted to forest, mountain or desert conditions, can mostly get along quite

China's endangered species: snow leopard, giant panda, and tiger

happily. Nevertheless, habitat destruction for industrial, housing, and recreation use continues, while pollution and hunting remain potent threats.

**Endangered Species**

Not even the star of China's wildlife show, the giant panda, is immune. This symbol of the World Wide Fund for Nature suffers from climate change, habitat loss, and reliance on a single food source: bamboo shoots. Fewer than a thousand remain in the wild, mostly in 11 nature reserves in Sichuan province (*see p132*). The Chinese authorities take stern measures against

hunters, including execution, but the survival of this striking black-and-white animal remains in the balance.

Other threatened species include the golden-haired monkey, Père David's deer, the snow leopard, the spotted-cat, the pangolin (scaly anteater), the giant salamander, and several species of crane. The three species of tiger – the Bengal, South China, and Manchurian – are almost extinct. The Yangtze river crocodile and Yangtze river dolphin are both protected species, but that does not stop them being threatened by pollution, sedimentation, fishing nets, and collisions with boats.

# National Parks

With a huge population, and a booming, but still underdeveloped economy, the Chinese have opted for a get-rich-first lifestyle, after which they may think about protecting their environment. It is a curious fact that in a country so proud of an artistic and literary heritage extolling the love of natural beauty, even the most emblematic places are not safe from litterbugs who choke gardens, hills, and lakes with refuse.

The Five Colour Pool in Jiuzhaigou, Sichuan

On a larger scale this translates into a couldn't-care-less attitude to environmental pollution, particularly of air and freshwater sources, which are often poisoned with dangerously toxic substances. As with so many aspects of life in China, an infrastructure of well-meaning laws and administration certainly exists, but its use is dependent on lazy, and often corrupt, officials.

Despite these multiple handicaps, an array of around 300 national parks and nature reserves has been established, protecting about two per cent of China's land area. These are backed up by provincial and local initiatives, such as designated 'scenic areas', which may lack the resources and more rigorous controls of the national bodies, but add to the stock of at least partially protected zones.

## Panda People

Undoubtedly the best known internationally is the **Wolong Nature Reserve** (Wolong Ziran Baohuqu) near Chengdu in Sichuan province, designated an International Biosphere Preserve by the United Nations for its role in protecting the endangered giant panda. Other endangered species that call Wolong home are the snow leopard, golden monkey and golden langur, and the musk deer.

The **Zhalong Nature Reserve** (Zhalong Ziran Baohuqu), 280km from Qiqihar in Heilongjiang province, is an excellent spot for birdwatchers, as is the remote Qinghai Lake in Qinghai province, and the **Poyang Lake** in Jiangxi province.

Zhalong was China's first nature reserve, established as recently as 1979, an indication of how recently environmental protection was considered an issue in China. Its 210,000 hectares of wetlands are a permanent home or stopover for 180 bird species. These include eight of the world's 15 crane species, of which six are on the endangered list. One of them, the red-crowned crane, is an ancient symbol of longevity, and there are 500 in the reserve. Other species, such as storks, swans, geese, and herons, are best seen from April to September.

## Wild Places

**Qinghai Lake** (Qinghai Hu), China's largest saltwater lake, is surrounded by snow-tipped mountains and located 3,200m above sea level in remote Qinghai province. The **Bird Island sanctuary** hosts about 100,000 migrating birds, including geese, cranes, vultures, and Mongolian larks. Its Longbao Black-Necked Crane Sanctuary plays an important role in the preservation of this threatened species.

Trees are the main players at the **Changbaishan Nature Reserve** (Changbaishan Ziran Baohuqu) in Jilin province, on the border with North Korea, where 210,000 hectares of virgin forest are protected. The trees form bands of growth, depending on the altitude, and include white birch, Korean pine, dragon spruce, and fir. Above 2,000m the landscape is tundra, while in the valleys there are deciduous trees which attract tour groups for their autumnal colours.

At the opposite end of the country, near Nanning, on the border with Vietnam, the **Longrui Nature Reserve** (Longrui Ziran Baohuqu) is the home of the world's only population of white-headed langur monkeys, while the plant kingdom is represented by the equally rare golden camellia.

In Hunan province, in the southeast, is a complex of connected nature reserves known as the **Wulingyuan Scenic Area** (Wulingyuan Fengjingqu), a remote area of rugged cliffs and hills emerging from the subtropical forest. Among its caves and plunging streams are numerous hiking and rafting possibilities.

The lush greenery and rugged rock formations of Wulingyuan Scenic Area

# Remote China

The north and west of China represents one of the last great wilderness areas on earth. Scarcely populated, the terrain is almost uniformly harsh and unforgiving, and it achieves this with an awesome variety of extreme conditions: snow-capped peaks, deserts, savannah, scorchingly hot depressions, and fast-flowing streams.

Ta'er Lamasery identifies an important Buddhist site

## INNER MONGOLIA (Nei Menggu)

Two-thirds of Inner Mongolia consists of the broad grasslands from which the Mongol hordes of Genghiz Khan sprang forth to rampage across China, the Middle East and Europe in the 13th century. The remainder is desert and mountain. Today, Inner Mongolia (as distinct from the independent Republic of Mongolia to the north) is an autonomous region of China. The horsemen of the grasslands still exist and some still live in compressed sheep's wool tents called *gher* (or yurts), but nowadays these symbols of the ancient way of life survive largely as part of a burgeoning tourism industry. Most Mongolians, who are outnumbered five-to-one by Han Chinese and other nationalities, prefer to ride motorbikes and live in ordinary houses.

### Hohhot

Capital of Inner Mongolia, Hohhot is a base for organised tours of the grasslands, which means visiting a rural community and sleeping in a yurt. The **Inner Mongolia Museum** (Nei Menggu Bowuguan) has notable displays depicting the traditional lifestyle of the Mongolian people. Other points of interest in the city are the **Great Mosque** (Qingzhen Da Si) dating from the Ming dynasty and the **Five Pagoda Temple** (Wuta Si).

At Ejin Horo Qi, southwest of Hohhot near Dongsheng, the **Genghis Khan Mausoleum** (Chengji Sihan Lingyuan) is a modern building that also manages to be quite beautiful, with its elegant domed-roof pavilions. Whether or not it is really Genghis Khan who lies beneath, who can say?

## QINGHAI

A huge province in the centre of western China, Qinghai forms part of the Qinghai-Tibet Plateau. With an average altitude of 4,000m, this is the highest plateau in the world, and so it is known as 'the roof of the world' (it is getting higher at the rate of 10mm per year).

Qinghai is hemmed in by mountains: the Qilian Shan range to the north, the Kunlun Shan to the west, the Tanggula Shan to the south, and the Hengduan Shan to the east. The Yangtze (Chang Jiang) and Yellow (Huang He) rivers both have their sources here.

### Qinghai Lake (Qinghai Hu)

Situated 300km west of Xining, this is

China's largest saltwater lake, and an important bird sanctuary (*see p133*). About 100km long, the lake is far from easy to see in its entirety, but the most important bird-spotting sight is Bird Island in its northwestern quadrant. Thousands of migrating and breeding birds, including bar-headed geese and black-necked cranes, can be seen here between March and June.

### Xining
This provincial capital marks the starting point of the highway to Lhasa, in Tibet, the highest highway in the world. The railway through Xining does not yet make it this far, but is being pushed southwards to Lhasa from Golmud (centre of the province), and will be an advantage to tourism.

The city has some notable sights, such as the **Great Mosque** (Qingzhen Da Si) and the North Mountain Temple (Beishan Si). The **Ta'er Lamasery** (Ta'er Si), 40km to the south, dates from 1397 and was built over the birthplace of Tsong Kapa, founder of the Tibetan Buddhist Yellow Hat sect.

The splendid modern tomb of Mongol warrior, Genghis Khan, Ejin Horo Qi

The Potala Palace in Tibet stands resilient and proud in spite of turmoil in the region

## TIBET (Xizang)

The Qinghai–Tibet Plateau, with an average height of 4,000m, and the Himalayan mountains, rising to 8,848m at the summit of Everest, are the defining physical characteristics of Tibet. A distinctive Buddhist tradition, with the priest-ruler Dalai Lama at its head, and a society that, until recently, was rooted in the medieval world, are its defining social characteristics.

Unfortunately, Tibet's tranquil and ordered existence has been disrupted since 1951, when the once independent country was occupied by Chinese forces and subjected to a massive influx of ethnic Chinese. Periodic bouts of rebellion are ruthlessly suppressed.

Despite this sombre political background, Tibet exercises an almost talismanic effect on foreign tourists, even allowing for the difficulties of getting there and the physical difficulties involved in simply getting around on the 'roof of the world'.

## Lhasa

The capital city's altitude of 3,700m above sea level can make it forbidden territory for those prone to suffer from altitude sickness. The old Tibetan quarter of the city is an atmospheric, if somewhat odiferous, warren of narrow streets and alleys where you may see people spinning prayer wheels as commonly as they talk or walk in the street.

The highlight of any visit is the stunning 17th-century **Potala Palace** (Budala Gong), formerly the seat of government and residence of the Dalai Lama, before which pilgrims prostrate themselves. Almost as impressive is the **Jokhang Temple** (Dazhao Si), Tibet's most important religious building, dating from the 7th century AD, and containing a statue of the child Sakyamuni which the faithful believe was carved by the Buddha himself.

Outside the city, trips can be made to the **Everest Base Camp** at Rongbuk.

## XINJIANG

The Xinjiang Uygur Autonomous Region, China's largest and most westerly region, has a population of about 13 million, and shares borders with several former Soviet republics, as well as Mongolia.

The Uygurs are one of China's national minorities, a people of Turkic origin, mostly settled in Xinjiang, a territory that they share with 12 other minorities, including the Daur, Tajiks, Mongols, and Kazakhs. Anyone who really wants to 'get away from it all' might try hiking in the trackless **Taklamakan Desert** that occupies the region's southwest – not many do!

### Kashgar

A fabled city on the Silk Route, this is about as far west, and as isolated, as you can get in China. A three-day bus-ride from Urumqi leads to Kashgar's Sunday Market (Jiari Jishi), and the Islamic-looking Id Kah Mosque (Qingzhen Si).

### Turpan

This former oasis city on the Silk Road, 200km southeast of Urumqi, is best known for the nearby Turpan Depression, 154m below sea level.

### Urumqi

The capital of Xinjiang, this city of one million people can be reached by train from Beijing – a distance of nearly 4,000km. An undistinguished city set in the fabulously wild terrain along which the Silk Route once wound its way, Urumqi has a good museum, the Xinjiang Autonomous Region Museum (Xinjiang Weiwuer Zizhiqu Bowuguan), with displays on the local minorities.

The Heavenly Mountain (Tianshan) and Heaven Lake (Tianchi) are 115km east of the city. The lake is perched at an altitude of 2,000m and the weather can be bitterly cold, even in summer.

Kazakhs in their summer finery, Xinjiang

# Marco Polo and the Silk Route

Marco Polo (1254–1324) was a Venetian merchant and traveller whose account of his adventures in China, and at the court of the Mongol Emperor Kublai Khan, became the subject of one of the greatest of all travel books. As a result, aristocratic Europe became entranced with China and with Chinese products, such as silk and porcelain.

Marco Polo's father and uncle had already made one trading visit to Kublai Khan's court at Beijing, whose splendour was legendary. When they decided to return to China in 1271, they took the young Marco with them. Kublai Khan took him into his service as an envoy, and finally as governor of Yangzhou. Marco Polo left China in 1292, returning to Venice in 1295 and writing *Il Milione* (*The Million* – which was translated as *The Travels of Marco Polo*).

Some scholars have questioned whether Marco ever reached China. While much of his narrative describes real people, places and conditions in China at the time, there are glaring omissions, such as the Great Wall, foot-binding, printing, tea, and the Chinese script. Names are frequently given in Persian, raising the suspicion that his 'journey' was actually made through the pages of a contemporary Persian account, augmented by tales heard from Arabic traders.

## Silk Route

These traders would have reached China by means of the ancient Silk Route, linking Europe with the Far East by way of Central Asia. There were several branches to the route, but from the 2nd century AD onwards, the two most popular ran from the Kaiyuanmen Gate in Xi'an (called Chang'an at the time), across the Gobi Desert to Turpan, Tashkent and Samarkand (the summer route), or Kashgar and Baktra (the winter route), and thence to Baghdad and the Mediterranean.

Products and cultural ideas flowed in both directions. The main Chinese export was silk, which was highly prized by the emperors and wealthy citizens of ancient Rome. Imports included cotton, grapes and, more lastingly, the Buddhist religion, imported from India.

Marco Polo sailed from Venice to the court of Kublai Khan. Others took the land route along the Silk Route, staying in tents en route, as families still do

# Northeastern China

Formerly called Manchuria, this region covers a vast, mountainous, and sparsely populated territory in the provinces of Liaoning, Jilin, and Heilongjiang. Historically, its nomads took any opportunity Chinese weakness offered to cross the Great Wall and ravage the rich lands to the south. The last time this occurred was in 1644, when the Manchu ruler Shunzi seized control, establishing the Qing dynasty on the Throne of Heaven in Beijing.

Dalian, the booming port

The Manchus, a people of Tartar stock, were set on the road to glory by their ruler Nurhachi, who united the tribes and became Khan in 1616, ruling from his palace at Shenyang. In the 20th century, Manchuria became a symbol of China's weakness: under Russian military control from 1900, it fell to the Japanese in 1932, and became the base for their puppet-state of Manchukuo.

The northeast has much to offer visitors, but few infrastructural facilities to help them on the way. Warm in summer, the region is subject to viciously cold temperatures in winter.

## CHANGCHUN
The capital of Jilin Province was (in 1932–45) capital of the Japanese-dominated Manchurian state of Manchukuo. It was here that the last Qing dynasty emperor, Pu Yi, who had been forced to abdicate in 1911, was reinstated as emperor, ruling over Manchukuo as a Japanese puppet, only to be taken captive by Soviet troops at the end of World War II. Returned to China, he was given a course in political re-education, then worked as a gardener before his death from cancer in 1967. (Bertolucci's *The Last Emperor* was a cinematic recreation of his life.)

### Palace Museum of the Last Emperor Pu Yi (Weihuang Gong)
This palace served as the official residence of the last emperor during his time as the so-called ruler of Japanese-occupied Manchuria, although Pu Yi actually lived elsewhere. There are some memorabilia of Pu Yi, including his throne, photographs, and a room that was once occupied by one of his wives. *South of the railway line. Admission charge.*

### DALIAN
Dalian is a major port and a seaside resort situated on the Liaodong Peninsula which separates the Yellow Sea from the Liaodong Gulf. The city's harbour, once known as Port Arthur, was a Russian 'concession' until it was occupied by the Japanese. As a result of this, Dalian has a legacy of Tsarist and Japanese architecture to add to its scenic

location. Its beaches are crowded in summer, but there is much rugged and open coastline nearby.

## HARBIN
Situated on the banks of the Songhua river, the capital of Heilongjiang province is an industrial centre and railway junction. In January and February, the citizens take advantage of Harbin's sub-zero temperatures to hold their world-renowned, spectacular Ice Sculpture Festival.

### Heilong Jiang Provincial Museum (Heilongjiang Sheing Bowuguan)
There is not much to see here, although there are some interesting natural history exhibits, including a complete woolly mammoth skeleton.
*City centre, near the International Hotel. Admission charge.*

### Jilin
The site of a winter ice-sculpture festival to rival the more famous one at Harbin.

### Steam Locomotives
China's increasingly rare steam engines operate on the railway line that passes through Harbin.

### Sun Island Park (Taiyangdo Gongyuan)
On the opposite bank of the Songhua river from the unpromisingly named (and unimaginatively conceived) Stalin Park (Sidalin Gongyuan), the Sun Island Park is being developed as a summer and winter outdoor leisure centre. Extending to almost 4,000 hectares, it has a lake, parks, ornamental gardens, and forests.
*North bank of the Songhua River. Admission charge.*

The spectacular colours of an Ice Festival pagoda, Harbin

Gateway leading to the Imperial Palace, seat of the Manchu emperors

## SHENYANG

Capital of Liaoning Province, Shenyang is an industrial city, and a base for travellers wanting to get off the beaten track and explore parts of old Manchuria. It was the Manchus' capital from 1625 until they took Beijing in 1644, and established the Qing dynasty.

### East Tomb (Dongling)

This is the tomb of the Manchu ruler, Nurhachi, grandfather of Shunzhi, the first Qing dynasty emperor. Situated outside Shenyang, it encapsulates, in miniature, the style that the Qing emperors would later perfect in Beijing. *Located in a forest park about 8km east of Shenyang. Open: daily 9am–4pm in summer, 10am–3pm in winter. Admission charge.*

### Imperial Palace (Gugong)

Built in 1625–36 during the reigns of the pre-Qing dynasty rulers, Nurhachi and Abahai, the palace remained the Manchu seat until their transfer to the Forbidden City in Beijing. Manchu architectural norms dominate over Chinese ones in the complex, and the palace is small enough to get around easily, yet big enough to give a feeling of the Qing rulers' driving ambition. Among the most important structures are the Hall of Great Affairs (Dazhen Dian), the Pavilion of Ten Princes (Shiwang Ting), and the emperors' private apartments at the Palace of Pure Tranquillity (Qingning Gong). *In the old city. Tel: (024) 2484 2215. Open: daily 9am–4pm in summer, 10am–3pm in winter. Admission charge.*

## North Tomb (Beiling)

The spectacular tomb of Abahai, son of the Manchu Emperor Nurhachi, was completed in 1651, but has later Qing-dynasty additions. The 'sacred way', lined with animals carved in stone, is reminiscent of the more impressive imperial tombs around Beijing.

*Huanghe Rd. In the northern suburbs. Tel: (024) 8689 6294. Open: daily 8.30am–4pm in summer, 10am–4pm in winter. Admission charge.*

Overlapping roofscape of the Dragon Throne, Imperial Palace, Shenyang

# Shopping

China manages to combine a great variety of styles, price ranges, and standards in its shopping. By itself this is not so unusual, but the sheer range of shops, stalls, and markets that it takes to serve its vast population is awesome. Yet the country is no shoppers' paradise, as any traveller who has been deposited by their tour bus at the door of too many Friendship Stores will know.

A private enterprise sign

Even worse are guides who pursue their sales commissions beyond the call of duty, so that their favoured arts and crafts stores assume the same importance as Ming-dynasty palaces on one's itinerary. Sometimes the only thing to do is to protest by refusing to leave the bus.

Counterfeiting is big business in China. 'Designer clothes', 'antiques', and 'antiquities' are mass-produced in supposedly illegal factories (the Chinese authorities have done little to stamp them out). It is important to check carefully the quality of items before buying. Even genuine products can have flaws that the sales staff may try to disguise. Antiques – historic items not more than 180 years old, bought from official stores and stamped with an official wax seal – should be what they purport to be; those from street markets are less likely to be genuine.

Anything more than 180 years old is classed as an antiquity. Tourists are often targeted by touts trying to sell stolen antiquities. Exporting antiquities is a serious offence, and while it happens on a grand scale – an estimated 20,000 of the country's several million historic tombs are looted every year – penalties are severe. Chinese violators are regularly executed. In addition to the moral repugnance of plundering a country's past, the risks of being set up, cheated, or caught and imprisoned should be taken seriously into account by tourists.

Despite all these caveats, there are plenty of fine products and souvenirs that one can bring back from China, so even confirmed non-shoppers should take enough time to consider the possibilities. Haggling is essential and expected. Even in more sophisticated shops and department stores it does no harm to push for a discount, especially if you are buying several items.

Friendship Stores, where only foreigners are allowed to shop, are not as ubiquitous as they might seem, even though all travel guides will lead you there as a matter of course. They can, however, be very useful for visitors with limited time for shopping. They carry a wide range of Chinese goods, but prices are better in the private shops and markets.

## What to Buy

### Carpets and Rugs

Carpets and rugs made in minority nationality areas, such as Inner Mongolia, Urumqi, and Xinjiang have a good reputation. Almost as good, although the patterns are different, are products from factories in Beijing and Shanghai.

### Cloisonné

This enamelled metal, or occasionally ceramic, work is decorated with intricate patterns, in which the colours are separated one from the other by copper wires soldered to the surface. Beijing and its surroundings sometimes seem like one big cloisonné factory and shop, and the wide range of ornaments and vessels made are generally of good quality. Xi'an is also a big producer, but tends to be much more expensive.

### Fans

Chinese hand fans are much sought-after. Not a serious product, perhaps, but an excellent souvenir. Hangzhou and Suzhou are noted for pretty styles. The finest folding fans are made from fragrant sandalwood and black paper.

### Jade

Technically, jade is a semi-precious stone, usually green or white, that can be found as either of two distinct mineral species: the rare and often translucent jadeite, and the more common nephrite, which has a waxy lustre. Nephrite was being used in ornamental carvings and ritual objects in China as early as the 3rd millennium BC. Jadeite did not reach China until the late-18th century from Myanmar, where it is still mined under appalling conditions. The Chinese ascribe mystical powers to jade.

Whether you buy or not, souvenir hunting in the Panjiayuan market, Beijing, is enjoyable

## Kites

Intricate designs in kite form can be purchased almost everywhere. Beijing and Shanghai are good locations, but perhaps best of all is Weifang, in Shandong province, which is known as the home of the kite.

## Lacquerware

Lacquer is a hard, waterproof material made from the resin of the lacquer tree, which is native to China and Japan. It can be coloured, polished, and carved, and since ancient times it has been used to decorate wooden vessels and furniture in China. Most of the main tourist zones have heaps of lacquerware, both good and bad, for sale.

Brushes for the budding calligrapher, and a clay figurine (below) – a speciality of Tianjin

## Paintings and Calligraphy

Line, rather than light and shadow, forms the basic structural element in traditional Chinese painting, and deft brushwork was, and is, used to create works of great delicacy from the simplest of painterly ingredients. Chinese artists aim to capture the essence as well as the form of a subject, whether it be a flower or a river, or a gaggle of elegantly coiffed imperial concubines dining at table. The works on sale at tourist traps will fall a long way short of such ideals, but may still form an adequate souvenir of a visit to China. Brushes for making your own Chinese paintings are good buys, with those from Huzhou and Jiangsu having the best reputation, although they are available everywhere.

Calligraphy, the art of Chinese penmanship, is writing at its most formal and decorative. In early times, writing was achieved by making marks with a sharpened willow stick on to strips of bamboo. General Meng Tian is credited with inventing the brush made of hair during the Chin dynasty (221 BC–AD 220) when, whilst supervising the construction of the Great Wall, he saw a tuft of goat's hair stuck to one of the stones and tried to write with it. Calligraphic paintings, brushes, writing materials, and chops – name stamps used by artists to 'sign' their paintings (and by others to imprint their names on documents) – can all be bought and make satisfying souvenirs. Chop-makers will make you a personal stamp bearing the characters that equate to your surname.

## Porcelain

Usually, and appropriately, known as china, porcelain is a hard, thin, vitreous and translucent material, fired at high temperatures (*see pp118–19*). The best porcelain is considered to be as white as jade, as shiny as a mirror, as thin as paper, and as resonant as a bell. There are many regional styles, although most can be purchased all over China – Foshan is noted for Shiwan porcelain, Jingdezhen for blue-and-white, eggshell and celadon, Shantou for multi-coloured flower motifs, and Yixing for purple-coloured and unglazed wares.

## Silk

Silk production originated in China, and the country still provides much of the world's highest-quality silk. The fabric is renowned for its lustre and drape. Suzhou, Hangzhou, and Nanjing all have good reputations for their silk, and sell high-quality goods at reasonable prices. Suzhou is considered best for embroidered silk, and Shanghai for brocade. Silk can be bought by the metre, and in a vast range of made-up products, including scarves, blouses, ties, jackets, underwear, and handkerchiefs.

## Tea, Herbs, and Spices

Markets and shops in all Chinese towns and cities sell masses of fine and aromatic souvenirs, including ginseng, dried Sichuan peppers, and black, green, semi-fermented, and flower-petal teas.

Illusionistic embroidered silk (from the Silk Museum in Suzhou) is a fine example of the craft

A whole range of Chinese crafts is found in some markets

## Where to Buy
### BEIJING
Shopping facilities, and prices, are burgeoning in China's capital, adding to an already extensive range of places to purchase both international and locally made products.

### Beijing Jade Carving Factory
Often superb items are sold straight from the factory floor in the attached shop.
*11 Guangming Rd.*
*Tel: (010) 6712 8899, ext 3612.*
### CVIK Plaza
A high-tech shopping centre, located in a Chinese/Japanese joint-venture complex selling international brands.
*22 Jianguomen Wai Ave.*
*Tel: (010) 6512 4488.*

### Friendship Store
Everything Chinese under one roof (just about), including silk, gold and silver, jewellery, jade, diamonds, ivory carvings (it is illegal to import these into many countries), embroidery, cloisonné, carpets, ceramics, calligraphy, painting materials (as well as completed works), antiques, furniture, food, drink, and other delicacies.
*17 Jianguomen Wai Ave.*
*Tel: (010) 6500 3311.*
### Lufthansa Shopping Centre
Among Beijing's most popular major shopping centres.
*52 Liangmaqiao Rd.*
*Tel: (010) 6465 1188.*
### Parkson Department Store
Western-style department

## MARKETS
In Beijing, the **Bird Market** (at the Xizhimen crossroads underpass, near the Fuxingmen metro station) is a bustling place where many other things besides birds can be bought (open: daily from 7.30am).

Hongqiao **Farmers' Market** is the place for snakes, pearls, antiques, and toys. On Tiantan Lu, beside the Temple of Heaven Park, is another street market.

In Guangzhou (Canton), the **Qing Ping Market** sells all manner of goods. Some of the 'antiques' may even be genuine.

Shanghai's beautiful **Mandarin Gardens Bazaar**, also known as the Yuyuan Market, sells an officially estimated 16,000-plus items in more than 100 small shops.

Hong Kong's **Bird Market** is famous. **Stanley Market**, with stalls in the lower streets of Stanley, on the south side of Hong Kong Island, is also very popular.

store, with a full range of household goods and clothing, as well as a food court and an arts and crafts gallery.
*101 Fuxingmen Nei Ave.*
*Tel: (010) 6601 3377/7374.*
*Also on 38A Xueyvan Rd.*
*Tel: (010) 6205 2650.*

## CHENGDU
**Craft and Art Market**
Traditional Sichuanese products, antiques, and bric-à-brac.
*32 Zongfu Rd.*
*Tel: (028) 665 5345.*
**Song Xian Bridge Art Centre**
Good for souvenirs.

*Xi Jiao Huan Hua Feng Jing Area.*
*Tel: (028) 778 1133.*

## GUANGZHOU
**Friendship Store**
One of the easiest places to buy a range of gifts.
*369 Huan Shi Dong Rd.*
*Tel: (020) 8357 6628.*
**Jewellery Import and Export Company**
Good-quality jewellery at bargain prices.
*54–58 Daxin Rd.*
**Xi Hu Night Market**
Market stalls selling all sorts of goods at very cheap prices.
*Xi Hu Rd, off Beijing Rd.*

## GUILIN
**Guilin Antique Store**
Sells fake antiques, locally made pottery, bamboo carvings, stone exercise balls, porcelain, and embroidery, among a wide variety of other things.
*79 Zhongshan Zhong Rd.*

## HANGZHOU
**Hangzhou Department Store**
Although there is much more to do in Hangzhou than shop, this is a good place to check out local products.
*739 Jiefang Rd.*

Consumerism has made the Cultural Revolution a thing of the distant past

Everything the Chinese chef could possibly need

## HONG KONG
Hong Kong is a shopper's paradise.

**Chinese Arts and Crafts**
There are several branches of this large group which, as the name suggests, provides a full range of arts and crafts.
*China Resources Building, 26 Harbour Rd, Wanchai.*
*Tel: (0852) 2827 6667;*
*& Star House, 3 Salisbury Rd, Tsim Sha Tsui.*
*Tel: (0852) 2735 4061.*
**Harbour City**
With some 500 shops and 50 restaurants, Harbour City, on the Kowloon waterfront, might seem to obviate the need to go anywhere else. There are, however, dozens of such centres in Hong Kong.
*Ocean Terminal, Canton Rd, Tsimshatsui.*
**Peak Galleria**
The dramatic location may compensate for generally higher prices.
*Victoria Peak summit: can be reached via the Peak Tram.*
**Tai Pan Tailor**
Reasonable, good-quality tailoring.
*Shop F3, Queensway Plaza, Hong Kong.*
*Tel: (0852) 2529 8861.*
**Tai Ping Carpets**
For hand-knotted, custom-made, and very expensive carpets.
*Wing On Plaza, Tsim Sha Tsui East.*
*Tel: (0852) 2369 4061.*

**Y William Yu**
Using tailors exclusively from Shanghai, the store basks in a high reputation for custom-made menswear.
*46 Mody Rd, Tsim Sha Tsui.*
*Tel: (0852) 2369 2141.*

## MACAO
Macao has fewer outlets than Hong Kong, and is slightly less frenetic.

**Asian Artefacts**
Specialists in Chinese antiques, particularly furniture.
*25 Rua dos Negociantes.*
*Tel: (0853) 881 022.*
**Pérola do Oriente**
For Chinese arts and crafts and furnishings.
*32 Avenida do Conselheiro Ferreira de Almeida.*
*Tel: (0853) 592 832.*

## KUNMING
**Kunming Department Store**
In the same premises as the Kunming Friendship Store, this is a good location for souvenir shopping, particularly for minority nationality products, such as handicrafts, and tin and copperware.
*99 Dongfang Xi Rd.*
*Tel: (0871) 316 4698.*

## NANJING
### Pearl Store
Otherwise known as the
Meijun Arts and Crafts
Department Store, this
shop sells a wide range of
high-quality souvenirs.
*Xuanwu Park.*
*Tel: (025) 663 9987.*

## SHANGHAI
Nanjing Dong Road is
perhaps the most famous
shopping street in China,
the pride of a city that
sees itself as the advance
guard of the new
cosmopolitan prosperity.
### Duoyunxuan
### (Stationery Shop)
Established in 1900,
this famous traditional
Chinese shop deals in
paintings and calligraphy,
and in the materials
needed to produce them.
*422 Nanjing Dong Rd.*
*Tel: (021) 6322 3410.*
### Friendship Store
Tourist-friendly, offering
souvenirs and gifts, as
well as groceries. Foreign
exchange on the premises.
*6 Zunyi Nan Rd,*
*Hongqiao.*
*Tel: (021) 6270 0000.*
*40 Beijing Dong Lu.*
*Tel: (021) 5308 0600.*
### Shanghai Antique Store
A vast emporium dealing
in antique paintings,
calligraphy, embroideries,

seals and ink-stones,
porcelain and jade.
Individual items, and
their prices, range from
the diminutive to the
gargantuan, and all
are stamped with a wax
seal to permit their
export.
*194–226 Guangdong Rd.*
*Tel: (021) 6321 4697.*

## SUZHOU
### Arts and Crafts Trading
### Centre
Local styles in fine
embroidery, jade carvings,
and lacquerware are
found here.
*568 Renmin Rd.*
*Tel: (0512) 727 1967.*
### Suzhou Silk Garments
### Factory
Demonstrates the art of
silk making, and houses a
store which sells a good
range of clothing and silk
goods.
*46 Lujia Xiang.*
*Tel: (0512) 729 8342.*

## WUXI
### Antique Store
For officially stamped
antiques.
*20 Tushuguan Rd.*
*Tel: (0510) 586 7425.*
### Friendship Store
The principal tourist
shopping store.
*8 Zhongshan Rd.*
*Tel: (0510) 544 0544.*

### Jiankang Chinese
### Pharmacy
Sells herbs, spices, and
traditional Chinese
medicines.
*428 Zhongshan Rd.*
*Tel: (0510) 524 327.*

## XI'AN
### Arts and Crafts Studio
More willing to bargain
than most.
*19 Yanta Rd.*
*Tel: (029) 7251 607.*
### Xi'an Cloisonné Factory
Good-quality pieces,
though Xi'an generally
is an expensive place
to shop.
*33 Dong Lu.*
*Tel: (029) 7210 005.*

A busy Shanghai market

# Entertainment

Nightlife is a relatively new concept in the People's Republic, although some cities in the 1920s and '30s such as Shanghai and Canton, were noted for their riotous jazz clubs, bars, gambling dens, and brothels. During the Cultural Revolution, only officially sanctioned forms of entertainment were allowed. Since the death of Mao, entertainment has blossomed. Western-style arts are becoming increasingly popular with affluent young Chinese. World-renowned performers are being lured to the cultural centres of Beijing, Guangzhou, and Shanghai, where forms of entertainment now rival any foreign city.

In addition to Chinese pop music the Western style has a strong following, and often provides the background for Chinese lyrics

## Bars and Cafés

### BEIJING

**Paulaner Brauhaus**
German pub with large beer steins.
*Kempinski Hotel, 50 Liangmaqiao Rd.*
*Tel: (010) 6465 3388.*

**Frank's Place**
A relaxed, but far from laid-back, American bar, popular with expatriates.
*Gongrentiyuguan Dong Rd. Tel: (010) 6507 2617.*

### GUANGZHOU

**Cafe Elles**
Popular haunt of expatriates and foreign visitors to Guangzhou.
*2/F Hua Xin Building, 1 Shui Yin Rd.*
*Tel: (020) 3760 4909.*

### HONG KONG

**Carnegie's**
Favourite drinking establishment, fun and friendly.
*9/F Lockhart Rd, Wanchai.*
*Tel: (0852) 2866 6280.*

**Club 97**
Cool crowd hang-out.
*24–26 Lan Kwai Fong, Central.*
*Tel: (0852) 2810 9333.*
*Branch in Shanghai.*

## Casinos

### MACAO

**Hotel Lisboa Casino**
The biggest casino in Macao.
*Avenida da Amizade.*
*Tel: (0853) 577 666.*

**Macao Palace**
This is a twin-deck ferry converted into Macao's second biggest casino.
*Inner Harbour.*

## Cinema

### BEIJING

**Capital Cinema**
Occasionally shows Western films.
*46 Xichangan St.*
*Tel: (010) 6605 5510.*

### HONG KONG

**Hong Kong Arts Centre**
A multi-screen complex showing international (mostly American) films as well as some of the better Hong Kong productions.
*2 Harbour Rd, Wanchai.*
*Tel: (0852) 2582 0232.*

## Classical Music and Opera

### BEIJING

**Beijing Concert Hall**
A principal venue for concerts by both visiting and home-grown orchestras.
*Bei Xinhua St.*
*Tel: (010) 6601 8092.*

### HONG KONG

**Hong Kong Arts Centre**
Halls in the complex are used for live music and opera performances.
*2 Harbour Rd.*
*Tel: (852) 2582 0232.*
**Hong Kong Cultural Centre**
Ultra-modern home of the Hong Kong Philharmonic and visiting orchestras.
*10 Salisbury Rd,*
*Tsimshatsui.*
*Tel: (852) 2734 9009.*

### GUANGZHOU

**Sun Yatsen Memorial Hall**
Superbly designed concert hall and venue for theatre and dance.
*Dongfeng Zhong Rd.*
*Tel: (020) 8355 2430.*

### SHANGHAI

**Shanghai Concert Hall**
For performances of classical works, both Western and Chinese.
*Yanan Dong Lu.*
*Tel: (021) 6386 9153.*

## Discotheques

### BEIJING

**JJ's Disco**
A very popular disco for the younger crowd.
*74 Xinjiexou Bei Ave.*
*Tel: (010) 6607 9691.*
**Zhongshan Park**
A great place for dancing.
*Zhongshan Park,*
*Changan Ave, off*
*Tiananmen Square.*

### HONG KONG

**Joe Bananas**
Trendy dance venue; no cover charge.
*23 Luard Rd, Wanchai.*
*Tel: (852) 2529 1811.*

### SHANGHAI

**Real Love**
Packed every night.
*10 Heng Shan Lu.*
*Tel: (021) 6474 6830.*
**Rojam**
International DJs here.
*4/F Hong Kong Plaza,*
*283 Huai Hai Zhong Rd.*
*Tel: (021) 6390 7181.*

Nightclubs jostle with late-night shops in Hong Kong's Wanchai district

The Chinese symphony orchestra

## Karaoke

Also known as KTV, karaoke bars are sprouting fast. Some charge foreigners outrageous prices for drinks.

### BEIJING
**Butterfly Karaoke**
Western tunes available, popular with young Beijingers.
*40 Xiaoliang Maqiao.*
*Tel: (010) 6466 3311, ext 384.*

### HONG KONG
**Point After**
The roster includes Western songs.
*Ambassador Hotel, 26 Nathan Rd, Tsim Sha Tsui.*
*Tel: (0852) 366 6321.*
**Regal Hong Kong Hotel**
High-class karaoke with lounge and rooms.

*88 Yee Wo St, Causeway Bay.*
*Tel: (0852) 2736 0922.*

### MACAO
**Karaoke Lounge**
Macao, too, has karaoke fever and this is a good place to experience it.
*Hotel Royal, 2–4 Estrada da Vitoria.*
*Tel: (0853) 2736 0922.*

## Live Music and Cabaret
### BEIJING
**CD Café Jazz Club**
Local jazz and rock music with impromptu visits from Chinese 'stars'.
*Dongsanhuan Rd, south of Agriculture Exhibition Centre, Chaoyong.*
*Tel: (010) 6501 8877.*
**Salsa Cabana**
Live Latin and salsa music. Lively crowd.
*1/F Kempinski Hotel.*

*Tel: (010) 6465 3388, ext 5700.*

### HONG KONG
**Jazz Club & Bar**
The best of local and international jazz combos pass through this busy club.
*34–36 D'Aguilar St, Lan Kwai Fong, Central.*
*Tel: (0852) 2845 8477.*
**JJs**
A hotel nightspot that manages to rise well above the usual level.
*Grand Hyatt Hotel, 1 Harbour Rd, Wanchai.*
*Tel: (0852) 2588 1234.*

### SHANGHAI
**Peace Hotel**
The Peace Hotel Jazz Band, composed mainly of gentlemen of mature years (as it has been since the 1920s), regales patrons of the lounge bar.
*20 Nanjing Dong Rd.*
*Tel: (021) 6321 6888.*

## Nightclubs
### HONG KONG
**Club BBoss**
An extravagantly large hostess club; one of the hottest nightlife venues in town.
*New Mandarin Plaza, 14 Science Museum Rd, Tsim Sha Tsui.*
*Tel: (0852) 369 2883.*

## MACAO

**Crazy Paris Show**

A must-see in Macao, this deliciously wicked (but not too wicked) can-can show takes place twice daily (three times on Saturday).
*Mona Lisa Hall, Hotel Lisboa, Avenida de Amizade.*
*Tel: (0853) 577 666.*

## SHANGHAI

**California Club**

The cool in-crowd place in town.
*Shanghai International Trade Centre, 2200 2 Gao Lan Rd, In Fuxing Park.*
*Tel: (021) 6318 0785.*

## Theatre

## HONG KONG

**Academy of Performing Arts**

Although an educational institution, APA is also a multi-disciplinary performance centre and one of the main venues for the annual Hong Kong Arts Festival, held from mid-January to the beginning of February.
*1 Gloucester Rd, Wanchai.*
*Tel: (0852) 2584 8500.*

**Fringe Club**

As the name suggests, it offers a mixture of alternative theatre and offbeat performances.

*2 Lower Albert Rd, Central.*
*Tel: (0852) 2525 7949.*

**Hong Kong Arts Centre**

Serious theatre and films, as well as an art gallery. Features Chinese and international artists and performers.
*2 Harbour Rd, Wanchai.*
*Tel: (0852) 2877 1000.*

## Traditional Chinese

## BEIJING

**Chaoyang Xiyuan**

Regular performances of the colourful art of Chinese acrobatics.
*36 Dongshanhuan Bei Rd, corner of Chaoyang Bei Rd. Tel: (010) 6507 2421.*

**Lao She Chaguan**

Professional cabaret and arias in a Beijing teahouse ambience.
*3rd Fl, Dawancha*

*Building, 3 Qianmenxi Ave. Tel: (010) 6303 6830.*

**Liyuan Theatre**

The Peking opera here makes some concessions to tourists' concentration levels and staying power.
*Qianmen Hotel, 175 Yongan Rd.*
*Tel: (010) 6301 6688.*

**Tianqiao Lechayuan**

A beautiful Beijing teahouse and an excellent place to see magicians, cabaret performers, and operatic extracts.
*13 Tianqiao Shichang.*
*Tel: (010) 6304 0617.*

## SHANGHAI

**Shanghai Circus World**

Chinese acrobatic performances.
*2266 Gong He Xin Rd (by Da Ning Rd).*
*Tel: (021) 5665 3646.*

Stars of the Chinese theatre

C hinese drama, including what is known abroad as Peking opera, began rather late in China's cultural evolution, during the Yuan dynasty (1279–1368), though it drew on older storytelling traditions.

Peking opera (which is only one of 300 different forms of traditional opera) only really flowered during the Qing dynasty, from the 18th century. It is characterised by exaggerated and stylised actions (generally perfomed by men), and high-pitched singing, accompanied by a piercing string and percussion ensemble. It is not to everyone's taste, although it is interesting to see at least once. The themes are usually romantic in the

broad sense, with characters using their skill to overcome natural disasters, rebellion or some other calamity. The high-pitched singing and music styles developed out of the need to project over chattering crowds in such noisy performance venues as markets and teahouses. Authentic Chinese opera is still a form of street theatre, but you can also see it in the more formal context of the theatre. Visually, the costumes are the most striking feature, and the style of the clothes, and of the make-up, all give clues to the characters' true nature.

## Circus

Chinese circus does not involve animals, and is all about acrobatics, performed by troupes and individuals whose skills are legendary. Plate-spinning and performing handstands on a pagoda of chairs are the least of their marvels. These skills originated with popular street theatre, and are emblematic of religious festivals, sacrificial rites, and themes from daily life, though they have since moved to the more sophisticated venue of the gymnasium. Acrobatics have a long history in China, although the first state acrobatic troupe was not formed until 1950, in Beijing.

Chinese opera is a highly stylised art, appreciated by few, but everyone enjoys the circus

# Children

China is not an ideal place for children. Even for adults, the rigours of independent travel test their stamina and patience. Organised tours are easier, but they may prove boring to most children. Some parents clearly decide that, since they want to see China, the children will have to as well, but most leave them at home.

## Amusement Parks

More and more Western-style amusement parks are appearing in larger cities – aquarium parks with dolphin shows, and pools with flumes and wave machines, interactive learning areas, and play parks with slides, mazes, and ball pits. Most parks have at least one such place for parents to deal with temple-sated children.

## Entertainment

Chinese opera, of interest to lovers of the art form, may also interest older children, and certainly the excellent Chinese circus should attract them all.

Colourful dances and re-enactments of traditional festivals may hold their attention for a while, but on organised tours they may see too many of such things for the novelty to last.

## Zoos

These are a bone of contention for many foreign tourists who have seen rose-tinted TV images of pandas in Chinese zoos, and are then shocked by the reality of the grim concrete-and-iron animal prisons. Children are natural zoo fans, but many children are also aware of animal rights and feelings, and they may not find the zoos appealing (nor the Chinese habit of throwing sticks and stones at the animals to make them 'perform').

## Safety

In the rush for economic growth, safety standards taken for granted in the West are often neglected – until it is too late. China is no stranger to disastrous accidents, whether in discotheques gutted by flames, or in buildings and tourist attractions that

## ONE-CHILD FAMILIES

Faced with the need to slow down the growth in China's population, the government adopted a 'one child per family' policy. Large families are traditionally seen as a source of security for parents' old age, and this meant a traumatic change in lifestyle. One side effect has been female infanticide, as parents try to ensure that the one child they are permitted is a male (women are still regarded as second-class citizens, especially in rural communities). Ironically, China is also worried that pampered single children, or 'little emperors' as they are known as, are growing up as a spoiled generation.

collapse on their occupants. While such things can, and do, happen in any country, poor maintenance adds appreciably to the risk, and is something that should perhaps be taken into account by parents when allowing their children to use amusement park rides, monorails, and adventure games.

## Cycling

While it is relatively safe to cycle in dedicated lanes, cycling becomes hazardous whenever heavy traffic is encountered, as it will be at every intersection. It takes time to grow accustomed to cycling in the kind of crowds that China generates, and constant vigilance is required to remain safe. Children should always be accompanied by an adult cyclist.

## Children's Palaces

These after-school community centres or youth clubs are designed for children and teenagers from the age of 7 to 16. Shanghai is well-endowed with such institutions, often housed in former colonial mansions. Selected children study arts, science, music, and sport. Foreign children can visit the Children's Palace at 64 Yanan Road (*tel: (021) 6249 8661*) on Tuesday and Saturday afternoons during the school term.

A gaggle of ducks offer boat rides at Behai Park, Beijing

# Sport and Leisure

The Chinese estimate that 300 million of their citizens take part in some form of sport, and that 70 million meet the sporting standards and criteria established by the state. They begin early, at school, where sport is considered a key part of the curriculum, with the best participants selected for special courses.

Gymnastics is taught from a very early age

Before Liberation in 1949, China had participated three times in the Olympic games and won nothing. A foreign newspaper caricatured the country with a cartoon showing a Chinese athlete staring at a duck's egg beside the Olympic symbol. Few people mock any more. At the 2000 Olympic Games in Sydney, China won 28 gold, 16 silver, and 15 bronze medals. China has won the bid to host the 2008 Olympics. Sporting achievement ranks alongside economic development and the space programme as an indicator of national pride and confidence.

The Chinese have made certain sports virtually their own. Gymnastics is one example, and ping pong, or table tennis, is another. Chinese players have developed a style of play where they throw the table tennis ball high in the air (so high that it seems they could read the *People's Daily* from cover to cover while waiting for it to return) then send it curving wickedly across the table. Many other sports of mainly Western origin are becoming popular in China. These include soccer (there are even soccer riots and hooligans), athletics, squash, badminton, tennis, and now golf (at an early stage of development).

## Traditional Sports

Martial arts (*wushu*), more commonly known as *kung fu* in the West, belongs to a tradition stretching back for thousands of years. Chinese wrestling, *tai chi* (*see box*), and *qigong* (a fitness exercise aimed at controlling the mind and regulating breathing to improve overall health and physiology) are other

## TAI CHI

Called *taijiquan* in Chinese, this is better known as *tai chi* in the West. It consists of a set of movements designed to exercise the body and mind. The aim is for the mind to control the movements of the body, which are graceful and gentle but complex.

Many Chinese begin their day with a *tai chi* session in a park or in the street, and there is a restful, almost mesmerising quality to the sight of hundreds of people moving to the natural rhythm of this exercise, which was formalised in the 17th century. People all over the world practise *tai chi* today.

examples of traditional Chinese sport. Then there are numerous minority nationality sports, including Mongolian-style wrestling and horsemanship, Tibetan yak racing, Korean acrobatics using a springboard, and the Miao crossbow competitions.

## Participatory Sports

Several of the top hotels in Beijing, Shanghai, and Guangzhou (Canton) have fitness centres, a swimming pool, and tennis courts. Non-residents can often use the facilities by paying an entrance fee or by becoming a member of the hotel's club. Golf has begun in a modest way in the Beijing environs; the most favourably situated course is that of the Beijing International Golf Club (*tel: (010) 6974 5678*). Adventure sports, such as bungee jumping, paragliding, and rock climbing, are becoming popular with the younger generation.

## Hong Kong and Macao

Hong Kong, as might be expected, has a full range of sporting facilities, both for spectators and participants. Horse racing at Happy Valley is immensely popular (*information available from the Hong Kong Tourist Office*). Macao is noted for its horse racing and its annual Formula 3 motor racing grand prix.

Tai Chi is both a graceful and meditative exercise

# Chinese Medicine

During the Ming dynasty, female herbalists – reputed to be witches – from Guizhou province in southwest China, concocted a wicked brew that could entrap men in matrimony. Today, most herbalists are engaged in the far less sinister task of trying to cure the everyday afflictions of the human condition, such as haemorrhoids, impotence, insomnia, eczema, and even old age.

Guizhou remains at the centre of the Chinese medical world, the source of many medicinal plants that grow abundantly in its hills, forming the basic ingredients of a medical revolution. From Guizhou comes a cure for haemorrhoids that involves dissolving a herbal powder in water and sitting in it for 30 minutes while the problem vanishes. It seems too good to be true, and it probably is, yet the market for this and other cures is booming. One Guizhou company reportedly makes around US$30 million a year selling herbal sperm regeneration powders and herbal aphrodisiacs, while it is playing the other side of the procreation market by trying to develop a herbal contraceptive.

## The Alternate Way to Health

Traditional Chinese medicine has a 2,000-year legacy and is favoured by a quarter of humanity for its supposed efficacy. The first official pharmacopoeia was produced in AD 659. New 'traditional' medicines are being added to the doctor's armoury all the time. Unfortunately, some of the alternate medicines rely heavily on animal

products. Today organisations like WWF are working with traditional Chinese medicine practitioners to encourage them not to use the bones and horns of endangered species such as tigers. Acupuncture, in which needles are inserted at key nerve centres in the skin, and reflexology are among the better-known techniques and are said to be effective against a wide range of conditions, including rheumatism, travel sickness, and the common cold.

Chronic ailments are often treated with herbal remedies, which are said to have fewer side effects than Western-style drugs, and simple complaints like colds can be ameliorated in the same way. For acute conditions, especially those requiring surgery, modern techniques are likely to be more reliable.

As in all traditional societies, herbalists and alternative practitioners use a variety of ingredients to effect their cures

Chinese cooking is a delicate, refined art

# Food and Drink

At its best, Chinese food represents the essence of the country's millennia-old culture, though it is wrong to think in terms of one monolithic 'Chinese cuisine'. Instead, there are several regional and local styles which have retained their identity while spreading around the country, and even across the world.

Attitudes in the People's Republic have changed since 1949, when the Communist Party considered gourmets to be 'enemies of the people'. While not all Chinese are gourmets, it is rare to find one that does not enjoy food. They can do so with a clear conscience and on the very best of authorities – Confucius himself pointed out that 'eating is the first happiness'.

Choose your kebab and watch it being cooked

To experience the delights of Chinese food in full, it is not enough to choose something comfortingly familiar, such as sweet-and-sour pork, hoping that it will taste the same as in the corner restaurant back home. It may well do so, but this misses the point of a Chinese meal, with its yin-yang balance of flavours, textures, and ingredients. Normal practice amongst Chinese is for one diner to act as 'leader', choosing from the dozens or even hundreds of dishes on offer, on behalf of all the other diners. Since the Chinese eat and enjoy everything, there are no problems of squeamishness or dislikes for the choice-maker to take into account.

## Pleasant Breaks
This is not to say the Chinese do not also enjoy fast food. On the contrary, street stalls sell an appetising array of soups, noodles, rice, or *dim sum* dishes for consumption at all times of the day. Yet people prefer to relax over their food whenever possible, and the low-cost and friendly restaurants of the new China are a far cry from the communal canteens favoured by Chairman Mao. Eating out has the added advantage of

giving people a break from their crowded apartments.

For many reasons, tourists are often starved of the chance to experience the full majesty of Chinese cuisine in a two- or three-week stay. Apart from a few prearranged 'banquets', organised tours generally opt for caution and convenience, as well as patronising those restaurants, good or bad, where their guide gets a 'commission' for bringing in the customers. Such caution is evident in the selection of dishes. These are mostly bland, although, to be fair, that is the way most tourists seem to prefer it.

### Escape to Taste

Other factors play a part, including concerns about hygiene and worries about upset stomachs which can make a misery out of a tightly scheduled itinerary. Nevertheless, if you do not take your courage in hand, click your chopsticks together a few times to satisfy sceptical Chinese diners that you can operate them, and plunge head first, so to speak, into real Chinese food, you cannot say that you have understood and savoured the taste of China.

At the very least, it is important to escape from the group occasionally and take your chance with the local restaurants – with a guide if possible, but without one if needs be. Restaurants range from simple street kitchens (where the quality in terms of taste, if not in style, is often fantastic) to high-priced restaurants (where the reverse is sometimes the case). More usually, the relationship between price and quality is a direct one. Between the two extremes is a growing middle sector, partly privately-owned and partly state-owned. The state sector tends to operate more restricted hours than the private, but is often preferred by ordinary Chinese for reasons of cost.

Food sold from street kitchens is cheap and delicious, and is usually freshly prepared while you wait

Exotic array of light foods

## FOOD AND DRINKS STYLE

Dog meat, chicken's feet, fish-heads, snakes' gall-bladders, bear's paw – so many foreigners turn up their noses at fare a Chinese would be honoured to receive that they cannot be blamed for keeping these delicacies to themselves and isolating the 'guests' in a separate room in the restaurant. The full-scale banquet is the highlight of Chinese cuisine, but there are many simpler highlights to be experienced every day.

### Peking Cuisine

Ducks could be forgiven for wishing this cuisine had never been invented, as they form a substantial part of its basic ingredients. Freshly roasted, crisp-skinned Peking Duck is famous the world over, and the many restaurants in the capital patronised by locals have to maintain high standards, because the Beijingese know what they like and stay away from what they do not. The skin and meat of the roasted duck are cut thinly and eaten in pancakes along with spring onions, cucumber, and sweet plum sauce. The meal ends with a soup made from the duck's carcass. As the north relies on wheat for its staple food, bread and noodles are more common than rice in Peking cuisine, and steamed dumplings are also popular.

### Cantonese Cuisine

'If its back faces heaven, you can eat it', goes a traditional Cantonese saying (a more modern version has it that the Cantonese will eat everything with wings, except for aeroplanes, and everything with legs, except the table). Guangdong province, source of Cantonese cuisine, is an extremely fertile area, yielding several harvests annually, and with a long coastline that provides an abundance of seafood. These fresh ingredients are mostly steamed or stir-fried, ensuring that their flavour and texture are retained. As a result they need little support in the way of spices or sauces, although light sauces of garlic, ginger, and scallions (green onion) are favoured. Rice is an important staple, coming from the subtropical hinterland. Snake is a local favourite, its taste being not dissimilar to that of chicken.

### Sichuan Cuisine

Spice is the variety of life in Sichuan, and the fiery taste of the province's cuisine, laced with red-hot peppers, is renowned throughout China. Visitors unfamiliar with how 'hot' food can get had better go easy with Sichuan food. The pepper varieties in Sichuan give food a sharp, lemony taste, which is different from the standard chilli flavour.

Although hot and spicy is the basic approach, the cuisine offers much more, and chefs work with a medley of seven tastes – sweet, sour, salty, fragrant, bitter, nutty, and hot – to get the balanced effect they are seeking. Sichuan's subtlety is present in tea-smoked and camphor-smoked duck, while tangerine-peel chicken, pork with vegetables, and bamboo shoots in a sweet sauce are delicately flavoured dishes.

## Hong Kong

Hong Kong is the citadel of Chinese cuisine. When Communism invaded the Chinese kitchen, people from all over the country fled to Hong Kong, bringing their culinary baggage with them and complementing the existing Cantonese

Spicy aromas of Sichuan cuisine

style. 'Have you had your rice yet?' is a traditional Hong Kong greeting. The city is a vast cornucopia of fine food, mostly Chinese of course, but with international flavours: all the Asian cuisines, and many European and American, are well represented. Hong Kongers lead hectic lives. Eating out is one of the pleasures they relish, and they have more than 30,000 eateries from which to choose.

Only a professional can make noodles

An ancient and charming custom – the Tea Ceremony

## Macao

Macao is distinguished by its Portuguese tradition, which is influenced in turn by the country's legacy of Moorish rule and its imperial connections with India (Goa), Africa, and South America. When Macaonese cuisine is added to a range of Chinese styles as extensive as Hong Kong's (although with a smaller choice of restaurants), dining out joins gambling as Macao's main attraction.

## Shanghai

Shanghai food, with its emphasis on seafood and subtle variations in taste, is one of the more notable local cuisines, despite being rather oily. Freshwater crabs, spiced baby eels, and freshwater shrimps cooked with Hangzhou tea, are all among the many items on the menu.

## Other Styles

In Muslim restaurants and households, particularly in the far west, mutton takes the place of pork, and pilaf rice is used in place of plain boiled. Hunan likes its spices, but uses them in a more restrained way than Sichuan. Around Guilin, steamed bamboo rat is a great delicacy, as is stewpot in Yunnan, and stewed chicken with ginseng in Jialing. Few dishes enjoy the exotic reputation of the Mongolian hotpot, which helps the northerners survive their long and harsh winters, and is in fact a kind of soup in which vegetables and meat

## CHINA AND TEA

Luk Yu, a Tang dynasty Master of Tea, wrote that drinking tea aids the digestion, especially 'when sipped in the company of sweet and beautiful maidens in a pavilion by a water-lily pond or near a lacquered bridge'. Most tea drinkers will not be so fortunate, but as long as the tea is good, they may be willing to make allowances.

Upholders of the finest traditions are the Luk Yu Teahouse in Hong Kong, and the Wuxing Teahouse in Shanghai's Mandarin Gardens and Bazaar.

In the Chinese tea ceremony, the miniature cups and teapot are doused with scaldingly hot water; tea is then placed in the pot, and boiling water added. After an appropriate interval, the tea is poured and drunk at once.

There are many varieties of Chinese tea, and though jasmine tea is usually served as a matter of course in restaurants, you could ask for black, fragrant green, linden, or magnolia tea instead.

are first cooked in boiling water at the table, and then eaten; the bouillon gradually becomes more flavourful, and is drunk at the meal's end.

## Dim Sum

'To touch the heart' is the literal translation of *dim sum*. Steamed in bamboo baskets or deep-fried, the ravioli-like dumplings, buns, pancakes, and other dishes that comprise *dim sum* are made with hundreds of different filling variations, including shrimp, pork, and sweet pastes. Typical *dim sum* houses are far from restful places: the press of people is vast and the noise level high. Waiters push heavily laden trolleys through the press. The only way to get the most out of the experience is to wade into the circus and shout and shove – in a friendly way, of course – along with everyone else.

## Beverages

Tea is the most popular drink in China (*see box*), but other beverages, some far less benign, are indulged in. Wines and liqueurs made from fruits, flowers, or herbs can be tasteful and sometimes potent drinks. Rice wines, particularly those from Zhejiang, have a good reputation. Beware of fiery *mao tai*, the national tipple, used in the *gan bei* ('bottoms up') toast at banquets (traditionally, the empty glass should be held upside down over one's head to show that the toast has been honoured; in fact, emptying the glass is not mandatory).

Chinese Beer, especially the light and fragrant lager-style Tsingtao (which is still brewed according to a 1930s German recipe), is of a high standard and is extremely refreshing with spicy foods.

The Chinese have raised the presentation of food to a fine art

## Where to Eat

All hotels have restaurants, most of which are very good. Street stalls can also be excellent, but watch for standards of hygiene. In the restaurant listings below, the following symbols have been used to indicate the average cost for two people, including wine.

| ★ | 100–150 RMB (cheap) |
| ★★ | 150–400 RMB (low to mid) |
| ★★★ | 400–700 RMB (mid to high) |
| ★★★★ | 700–1000 RMB (expensive) |

*(See p185 for conversion to HK$ and Macao MOP.)*

### BEIJING

The capital is acquiring all the advantages of a major international metropolis, including a restaurant sector well able to satisfy the tastes of tourists, business travellers, and foreign residents.

### Confucian Heritage ★★

Cuisine based on the style of Shandong province, in a traditional teahouse.
*3 Xiliulichang St. Xuanwu District.*
*Tel: (010) 6303 0689.*

### Debao Shijie ★★

A pleasant way to try Cantonese cuisine. Pick your own food; the waiter takes it to cook and serve.
*Debao Hotel, 22 Debao Xinguan Xizhimenwai Ave.*
*Tel: (010) 6831 8866, ext 2130.*

### Fangshan ★★★

Banquets in imperial style and ambience in the old imperial Beihai Park.
*Qionghua Dao (Jade Flower) Island.*
*Tel: (010) 6401 1879.*

### Hongbinlou ★★

Cuisine from China's Muslim minority, with the emphasis on mutton.
*82 Xichangan St. West of Tiananmen Square.*
*Tel: (010) 6603 8469.*

### Gong De Lin ★★

From the famous Shanghai vegetarian restaurant serving all veggie faux meat dishes.
*158 Qianmennan Day Ave, Chongwen District.*
*Tel: (010) 601 1915.*

### John Bull Pub ★★★

Sells British favourites like fish 'n' chips and steak and kidney pie.
*44 Guanghua Rd, Chaoyang District.*
*Tel: (010) 6532 5905.*

### Quanjude Roast Duck Restaurant ★★

Superbly atmospheric, if crowded. The capital's best

## CHOPSTICKS

Chopsticks can be awkward at first. Perseverance is needed to get the technique right, but a Chinese meal is best enjoyed with them, and the two sticks can be surprisingly agile in practised hands. The bottom stick is the 'anvil', held firmly between the first joint of the ring finger and the lower thumb, while resting in the crook of forefinger and thumb. The top stick is held like a pen between the tip of the thumb and forefinger, and pivots against the lower stick.

---

---

roast duck tops the menu.
*32 Qianmen Ave.*
*South of Qianmen Gate.*
*Tel: (010) 6511 2418.*

**Ritan Park ★**
Chinese snacks (such as steamed dumplings) in a leafy poolside ambience.
*Temple of the Sun Park (southwest). Near the Friendship Store.*
*Tel: (010) 6500 5883.*

**Sichuan Restaurant ★★★★**
Located in the former mansion of a Qing-dynasty prince, this renowned restaurant specialises in Sichuan-style banquets.
*51 Xirongxian Hutong.*
*South of Xichangan St.*
*Tel: (010) 6603 3291.*

**Debao Shijie ★★**
Busy but pleasant way to try Cantonese cuisine. Pick your own food and it is cooked for you.
*Debao Hotel, 22 Debao Xinyuan Xizhimenwai Ave. Tel: (010) 6831 8866.*

## CHENGDU
**Chengdu Restaurant ★★**
Good Sichuan cuisine.
*134 Shangdong Ave.*
*Tel: (028) 666 085.*

## GUANGZHOU
**Banxi ★★**
Set around a large pond, specialising in *dim sum.*
*151 Longjin Xi Rd.*
*Liwanhu Park.*
*Tel: (020) 881 5718.*

**Datong ★★★**
Enjoy *dim sum* and crispy fried duck while over-looking the Pearl River.
*63 Yanjiang Xi Rd.*
*Tel: (020) 888 8988.*

**Guangzhou ★★★★**
Meals are served in a flower-bedecked ambience on floors surrounding a courtyard.
*2 Wenchang Nan Rd.*
*City centre.*
*Tel: (020) 888 3888.*

**She Canguan ★★★**
Snake is the big thing at this establishment (otherwise known as the Snake Restaurant).
*43 Jianglan Rd.*
*Tel: (020) 888 3811.*

Snake restaurant – not for the faint-hearted

## HONG KONG

**Dan Ryan's Chicago Grill** ★★★
For Americans and others who love US cooking, this is one of the best.
*114 The Mall, Pacific Place, Queensway, Central.*
*Tel: (0852) 2845 4600.*

**Tandoor Indian Restaurant** ★★★
Some of the finest Indian food is served here.
*3/F On Hing Building, 18-20 Wyndham St, Central.*
*Tel: (0852) 2845 2299.*

**Hunan Garden** ★★★★
An elegant restaurant with prices to match, serving up the spicy taste of the Hunan province.
*3/F, The Forum Exchange Square, Central.*
*Tel: (0852) 2868 2880.*

**Jumbo Floating Restaurant** ★★★
More exciting for its views than its food, this water-borne eatery is set in boat-filled Aberdeen Harbour (free launches take diners there and back from various jetties).
*Aberdeen, on Hong Kong Island's southern coast, Shun Wan Wong Chuk Hang Rd.*
*Tel: (0852) 2553 9111.*

**Luk Yu Tearoom** ★★★
Almost a legend in itself, the Luk Yu serves a huge range of teas and *dim sum* in an atmospheric back-street restaurant; prices are added up using an abacus.
*24–26 Stanley St, Central.*
*Tel: (0852) 2523 5463.*

**Sichuan Garden** ★★
Moderately priced Sichuan dishes.
*3/F Gloucester Tower, The Landmark, Central.*
*Tel: (0852) 2521 4433.*

**Tsui Wah** ★
It would be hard to beat the taste or the prices at this Cantonese restaurant.
*15 Wellington St, Central.*
*Tel: (0852) 2525 6388.*

## KUNMING

**Meng Du** ★★
Cantonese and Sichuan-style food.
*2 Yongsheng Rd.*
*Tel: (0871) 313 0209.*

## MACAO

**Furusato** ★★★★
Both Japanese and Korean food are served in the restaurant of this notable architectural monument, the Hotel Lisboa.
*Avenida Infante Dom Henrique. Tel: (0853) 577 666, ext 1137.*

**Henri's Galley** ★★
Puts together a remarkable range and quality of styles – Portuguese soups, African chicken, Macao sole, and even a mean steak – in a simple 'sea dog' kind of ambience.
*4 Avenida da República.*
*Tel: (0853) 556 251.*

**Long Kei** ★★★
An ordinary looking Cantonese restaurant, but one where the food is a cut above the rest.
*7b Largo do Senado.*
*Tel: (0853) 573 970.*

## NANJING

**Dasanyuan** ★★★
Noted for its Cantonese specialities.
*38 Zhongshan Rd.*
*Tel: (025) 472 2779.*

**Baixing Renjia** ★★
Excellent value buffet, good for vegetarians.
*103 Zhongshan Bei Rd.*
*Tel: (025) 324 2282.*

## SHANGHAI

**Latina** ★★
Excellent all-you-can-eat BBQ buffet at reasonable prices with live Brazilian music at their Mao Ming Road branch.
*59 Mao Ming Nan Rd.*
*Tel: (021) 6472 2718.*
*Nos. 18–20, Lane 169, Tai Cang Rd, Xintiandi, Ma Dang Rd.*
*Tel: (021) 6320 3566.*

**1221** ★★★
Very classy, but not too expensive Shanghainese

eatery. Advance bookings are recommended.
*1221 Yan An Xi Lu.*
*Tel: (021) 6213 6585/2441.*
**Le Garçon Chinois**★★★
Continental and Chinese food in a lovely setting on three floors. The café/bar is on the first floor. The owner often brings out his saxophone to play some jazz.
*No. 3, Lane 169, 9 Heng Shan Rd.*
*Tel: (021) 6445 7970.*
**Fwu Luh Pavilion** ★★★★
Plush interior design. The restaurant serves both traditional and experimental Yangzhou cuisine. Worth a visit for the presentation of food and also the decor.
*No. 603B, Grand Gateway, 1 Hong Qiao Rd.*
*Tel: (021) 6407 9898.*

## SUZHOU
**Songhelou** ★★★
The 'Pine and Crane' restaurant claims a 200-year-old tradition, and states that the Emperor Qianlong dined there. It specialises in Suzhou dishes.
*141 Guanqian St.*
*Tel: (0512) 777 003.*
**Wangsi** ★★
Famed for its 'beggar's chicken', red osmanthus-flavoured glutinous rice, and other Suzhou specialities.
*23 Taijian Long.*
*Tel: (0512) 227 227.*

## XI'AN
**Changan Lu Canting** ★
A simple diner, popular with locals, good value.
*15 Changan Bei Rd.*
*Tel: (029) 751 316.*
**Qujiangchun** ★★★★
A taste of Tang-dynasty theatricals in the preparation and presentation of the meal.
*192 Jiefang Rd.*
*Tel: (029) 773 572.*

Hong Kong's Jumbo Floating Restaurant

# Hotels and Accommodation

Hotels in China present the full range of standards. Joint ventures with some of the world's leading hotel groups have led to the development of hotels in the major tourist and international business zones whose commitment to quality is impeccable. In fact, it is possible to make a case for saying that China's hotel standards are too high, with too many hotels targeted at the high end of the price range, leaving a dearth of reasonable quality hotels for travellers on a restricted budget.

Welcome to Peace Hotel

Travellers on a package tour will have a fair idea of what to expect, and the first few nights will be a good indicator of whether or not their expectations will be realised. Such tours are reliable, although there are bound to be some variations in a country as big as China. Nevertheless, in all but the top hotels, the slovenly practices of the staff (and of previous guests) can mar the stay.

In less well-run hotels, expect a whole gamut of problems. Count yourself lucky if the worst you experience is unwashed windows spoiling the view. Others will encounter stained and dirty, used sheets, toilets that run constantly, hot water that does not run at all, carpets seared by cigarette burns, stains, bare electrical wires, and ill-fitting power points. Complaints often have zero effect, but it is worth the attempt.

## Hopes and Dreams

Independent travellers will have far less chance of finding reasonable accommodation for a modest price. In many towns and tourist areas, there may be no alternative but to check into the expensive 5-star hotel. Lower-cost hotels do exist (although the standards of service and cleanliness are often miserable), but many accept only Chinese guests, and no amount of argument will alter this.

China's own people are becoming tourists as fast as they can. This represents a vast pool of travellers, and an equally vast pool of competitors for hotel rooms whose number may be inadequate at peak times. Advice to try staying at university dormitories is mostly useless, because Chinese students also like to travel and will be there ahead of you. All this forces foreign tourists into more expensive hotels, which is where the Chinese tourism authorities prefer to see them in any case.

## Hong Kong and Macao

Hong Kong represents a special case. There are few cities in the world where pressure on hotel space is so intense, where the response in terms of new construction is so inadequate, and where budget opportunities are almost non-existent. Even the YMCA and YWCA, usually far from the top of most international travellers' wish lists, can be besieged by business people and well-heeled tourists engaged in a frantic search for accommodation (both are, in fact, fairly high-standard and high-priced hotels). It is not uncommon for every single hotel room in Hong Kong to be booked, so make arrangements well in advance. Make best use of package deals, where the combined cost of air fare and hotel room is far lower than you could possibly negotiate for yourself. The situation is less critical in

Many luxury-class hotels are designed by international architects

Macao, except at weekends and during important race meetings, but the same general rule applies.

China's 5-star hotels are equal to the best in the world

Garden Hotel, Shanghai

## Star Ratings

The star rating system is a good, but not absolutely uniform, guide. Stars are awarded mostly on service quality, facilities, and hygiene, but political connections can influence allocation. Ratings of 1 to 3 stars are awarded by provincial authorities, with 3 stars having to be approved by the national tourism administration. Ratings of 4 and 5 stars can only be awarded by the national authority. In lower-rated hotels there will be a 'guardian' on each floor to keep an eye on things – and on you. Even in the top-rated hotels it is not recommended to drink tap water, unless there is a specific notice saying that it is safe to do so.

**No stars:** while much depends on the attitude of staff, the quality in such establishments is usually abysmal. No one would complain about spartan facilities, but these hotels tend to be extremely dirty and infested by a variety of insect life.

**1-star:** simple, but with air-conditioning, coffee shop, and a majority of rooms with private bath.

**2-star:** air-conditioned, most rooms with private bath, offering Western and Chinese breakfast.

**3-star:** fully decorated and well-equipped rooms, elevators, IDD telephones in rooms, television, in-house movies, 24-hour running hot and cold water.

**4-star:** deluxe, fully equipped rooms, with extras such as hairdryers, business centre, fitness centre, swimming pool, medical centre, and a range of restaurants and bars.

**5-star:** standards which match the very best in the world.

## Accommodation Categories
### Prices

Rates are usually based on bed-and-breakfast or on room-only rates per person, although fully inclusive package tours may include lunch and/or dinner. The state sets minimum room rates so it may not be possible to negotiate discounts. However, there is no harm in trying, particularly at quiet times.

### Business

In booming business destinations, such as Beijing, Guangzhou and Shanghai, hotel rooms may be hard to come by at precisely the same times of year that tourists are also competing for the available space. Continuing new construction should keep supply and demand in reasonable balance, but early booking remains essential.

### Deluxe (US$250 plus)

It is no accident that many hotels in this category have the word 'Palace' in their title. They may be a shade less palatial or perfect than the best international standards, but this is not necessarily a bad thing, as it leaves some space for at least a little Chineseness to slip through.

### Premier (US$150–250)

Business travellers generally opt for this level, which offers all the facilities they need for business and leisure, but with fewer crystal chandeliers than the best.

### Moderate (US$100–150)

Most ordinary package tours to China aim at this standard of hotel, which is perfectly acceptable for overseas visitors.

### Budget (US$30–100)

This is the ideal hotel category for budget travellers, combining relative cheapness with a reasonable standard of facilities, though not always of cleanliness.

### Cheap (below US$30)

Prices can be well below $30, but in general it is neither easy nor pleasant for foreigners to stay in such cheap accommodation. The Chinese prefer visitors to spend freely, and discourage them from using such facilities.

### Thomas Cook

Travellers who purchase their travel tickets from a Thomas Cook Network location are entitled to use the services of any other Thomas Cook Network location, free of charge, to make hotel reservations.

The foyer of the Jin Ling Hotel in Nanjing

# On Business

China was long seen by international business as the pot of gold at the end of the rainbow. Its potential market of over a billion consumers led to the inevitable thought: 'If only each Chinese would buy just one of my products ... '. More sober assessments have now taken over. China wants to export, not import, to acquire foreign technology, not buy ready-made products. It is also involved in wide-scale piracy, from computer programmes, video films and compact discs, to designer-label fashions and accessories.

Internet connections are easy to find in big cities

Nevertheless, China still represents the single biggest market in the world, and one that, starting from a low base, has consistently posted the fastest growth rates of any newly industrialising country. International companies have found that it is possible to make money in China, but only if the game is played by Beijing's rules.

China has no intention of allowing foreign multi-national corporations to dominate its economy. They can do business, and many do so with their own wholly owned facilities, but they mostly operate in joint ventures with Chinese partners.

'Joint ventures' – where foreigners provide the expertise and capital, and the Chinese provide cheap (and often highly trained) labour – are the magic formula for doing business in China, whether it be making hamburgers, or operating airliners. Joint ventures can be set up in cities and areas designated by Beijing as special economic zones, or as open cities for foreign investment. In

practice, while the government bureaucrats are trying to keep control of the reins, the reality is changing faster than they are able to deal with. Cities like Shanghai and Guangzhou (Canton) appear to make their own rules.

## Legal Loopholes

At the same time, the legal framework, designed for a Communist command economy, has had a hard time keeping up with the changes wrought by the fast-growing economy. Even where there are adequate laws in place, lax enforcement allows lawbreakers to operate with impunity. Corruption also plays a part, with government functionaries 'augmenting' their salaries, and members of the elite abusing their positions to amass fortunes. Occasionally someone is executed as an example to the rest, but graft is too deeply ingrained to be eradicated easily.

Perhaps the best hope lies with the Chinese workers, who are increasingly prepared to take independent action against corrupt officials, and against abysmal working conditions at locally owned and joint-venture enterprises.

## Doing Business

Beijing, Guangzhou (Canton), and Shanghai are the main venues for a vast array of international trade fairs, congresses and conventions covering everything from toys through sewage systems, to cars and aerospace. Progress is likely to be slow, as the Chinese do business as much on the basis of personal contacts as of contracts, though this is slowly changing.

It makes sense to discuss possible avenues of approach with business people whose organisations are already active in China, and a number of banks, accountancy firms, and agencies offer this service. Another approach is to contact the economic development office of your embassy in Beijing, or the appropriate chamber of commerce, to seek advice on likely possibilities and contacts.

## Useful Addresses
### BEIJING
**British Chamber of Commerce**
*Tel: (010) 8331 5013/5016.*
*bcc/gd@ihw.com.cn*
**China Council for the Promotion of International Trade**
*4 Fuxingmenwai St. Tel: (010) 6801 3344.*
**China Economic Development Corporation**
*93 Beiheyan Ave.*
**China International Trust & Investment Corporation (CITIC)**
*19 Jiangguomen Wai Ave.*
**China Investment Bank**
*Fuxing Rd.*

### GUANGZHOU (CANTON)
**Bank of China**
*193 Ghangdi Rd.*
*Tel: (020) 8333 0458.*
**British Chamber of Commerce**
*Tel: (020) 8331 5013.*
*bcc.gd@ihw.com.cn*
**External Economic Information Consultancy & Service** and **Guangzhou Administrative Bureau for Industry and Commerce**
*120 Liu Hua Rd.*
**Guangzhou Economic & Technical Development Office** and **Guangzhou Foreign Trade Corporation**
*120 Liu Hua Rd. Tel: (020) 666 9900.*

### SHANGHAI
**British Chamber of Commerce**
*Tel: (021) 6218 5183.*
*britcham-sh@online.sh.cn*
**China Council for the Promotion of International Trade**
*28 Jinglingxi Rd. Tel: (021) 6386 5572.*

New buildings, Dongchang'an Jie, Beijing

# Practical Guide

## Arriving
### Passports and Visas
All visitors to China must obtain a visa before arrival. Visas are issued by Chinese embassies and consulates, as well as by some offices of the China International Travel Service (CITS) and China Travel Service (CTS). They can be obtained at short notice from the CITS and CTS offices in Hong Kong and Macao. Rules are becoming less stringent, with three-month visitor visas available, extendable by application to the Public Security Bureau in China (*see* Police, *p186*).

## By Air
Most travellers arrive at Beijing, Guangzhou (Canton), or Shanghai international airport within a short distance of the city. Hong Kong's Kai Tak International Airport lies within the city; as well as the new airport on Lantau Island, with road and tunnel links to the city. Macao's international airport opened in 1997.

## Airport Tax
This tax is paid separately at a special counter before departure – in Hong Kong you pay the tax at the airline counter where you check in.

## Airport Transport
There are excellent taxi and bus links between city and airport at Beijing, Guangzhou and Shanghai, and at Hong Kong. Several hotels however, do offer a limousine and/or shuttle-bus service to and from the airport.

## By Sea
There are passenger services from Japan and South Korea to China, but most people arriving by sea do so by taking the ferry services from Hong Kong or Macao to Guangzhou (Canton). There is also a (slow) service linking Hong Kong and Shanghai.

## By Road
It is not possible to enter China by bus from Kazakhstan, Mongolia, Nepal, Kyrgyzstan, North Korea, Pakistan, Russia, or Vietnam (the situation with Myanmar and India remains uncertain). This is the hardest way to travel, especially in remote areas.

## By Rail
Most rail passengers arrive in China on the Hong Kong-Guangzhou express. More exotic routes, such as the trans-Siberian Express across Russia or Mongolia to Beijing, are also popular, while a new route from Kazakhstan to Xinjiang has recently opened.

## Camping
Camping in China requires a special permit. Travellers who pitch a tent in any convenient spot are likely to become 'guests' of the Public Security Bureau.

## Climate
The south is tropical, with warm conditions all year round (and often very hot and humid in summer). The north is baking hot in summer and freezing in winter, with a brief spring and autumn of clear, sunny weather.

Coastal regions are more moderate, but prone to seasonal rains and winds. The mountains and plateaux of the west can be very cold.

## Crime

Crime has not been much of a problem in the past in China, particularly against foreigners, and strong measures are taken against gangs preying on train travellers, for example. Pickpocketing, pilfering, and mugging are reportedly on the increase, but can be avoided with a few sensible precautions. City streets are safe and relaxed at night. Tourists are unlikely to be affected by crime in China.

## Customs Regulations

The duty-free limits are 2 litres of alcohol, 600 cigarettes, and 0.5 litres of perfume. There is a notional limit of 1,000m of video film and 72 rolls of still film. Unlimited amounts of foreign currency can be imported, but amounts above US$5,000 need to have been declared, and foreign exchange receipts retained if the balance is to be re-exported at the end of your trip. Chinese customs are tough with illegal narcotics and pornographic or

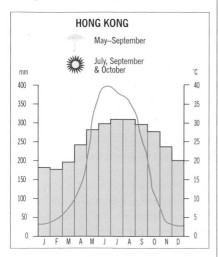

HONG KONG

☂ May–September

☀ July, September & October

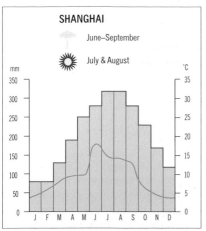

SHANGHAI

☂ June–September

☀ July & August

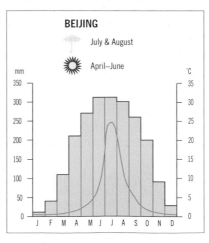

BEIJING

☂ July & August

☀ April–June

**Weather Conversion Chart**
25.4mm = 1 inch
°F = 1.8 x °C + 32

### Conversion Table

| FROM | TO | MULTIPLY BY |
|---|---|---|
| Inches | Centimetres | 2.54 |
| Feet | Metres | 0.3048 |
| Yards | Metres | 0.9144 |
| Miles | Kilometres | 1.6090 |
| Acres | Hectares | 0.4047 |
| Gallons | Litres | 4.5460 |
| Ounces | Grams | 28.35 |
| Pounds | Grams | 453.6 |
| Pounds | Kilograms | 0.4536 |
| Tons | Tonnes | 1.0160 |

To convert back, for example from centimetres to inches, divide by the number in the third column.

**Men's Suits**

| | | | | | | | |
|---|---|---|---|---|---|---|---|
| UK | 36 | 38 | 40 | 42 | 44 | 46 | 48 |
| Rest of Europe | 46 | 48 | 50 | 52 | 54 | 56 | 58 |
| US | 36 | 38 | 40 | 42 | 44 | 46 | 48 |

**Dress Sizes**

| | | | | | | |
|---|---|---|---|---|---|---|
| UK | 8 | 10 | 12 | 14 | 16 | 18 |
| France | 36 | 38 | 40 | 42 | 44 | 46 |
| Italy | 38 | 40 | 42 | 44 | 46 | 48 |
| Rest of Europe | 34 | 36 | 38 | 40 | 42 | 44 |
| US | 6 | 8 | 10 | 12 | 14 | 16 |

**Men's Shirts**

| | | | | | | |
|---|---|---|---|---|---|---|
| UK | 14 | 14.5 | 15 | 15.5 | 16 | 16.5 | 17 |
| Rest of Europe | 36 | 37 | 38 | 39/40 | 41 | 42 | 43 |
| US | 14 | 14.5 | 15 | 15.5 | 16 | 16.5 | 17 |

**Men's Shoes**

| | | | | | | |
|---|---|---|---|---|---|---|
| UK | 7 | 7.5 | 8.5 | 9.5 | 10.5 | 11 |
| Rest of Europe | 41 | 42 | 43 | 44 | 45 | 46 |
| US | 8 | 8.5 | 9.5 | 10.5 | 11.5 | 12 |

**Women's Shoes**

| | | | | | | |
|---|---|---|---|---|---|---|
| UK | 4.5 | 5 | 5.5 | 6 | 6.5 | 7 |
| Rest of Europe | 38 | 38 | 39 | 39 | 40 | 41 |
| US | 6 | 6.5 | 7 | 7.5 | 8 | 8.5 |

anti-government literature. Excessive amounts of religious literature are also grounds for suspicion. Chinese currency may not be taken out of the country.

### Cycling

Cycling is widespread in Chinese towns and cities, and is mostly safe. There is not much margin for error because of the congestion. Foreign mountain bikers and trek-bikers are not encouraged. Cyclists who go off the beaten track can expect to have their mounts 'detained' by the local Public Security officers.

### Driving
#### Roads

Because of the poorly developed national highway system, an all but non-existent car-hire sector, and the terrifying way in which most Chinese drive, few short-stay visitors will want to drive. For longer-term visitors, a special permit is needed.

#### Rental

Car hire has recently been introduced in Beijing and Shanghai, but on a very minimal basis. Cars with drivers can, however, be hired easily. Information on different hiring agencies is available from hotel desks and local CITS and CTS offices.

### Electricity

The electricity supply is 220 volts, 50 cycles AC. Several socket types are in use, for which a multiple adaptor plug should be purchased before departure.

## Embassies
Embassies in Beijing include:
**Australia** 21 Dongzhimen Wai St.
*Tel: (010) 6532 2331.*
**Canada** 19 Dongzhimen Wai St.
*Tel: (010) 6532 3536.*
**Ireland** 3 Ritan Dong Rd.
*Tel: (010) 6532 2691/2914.*
**New Zealand** 1 Ritan Dong St.
*Tel: (010) 6532 2931/3.*
**UK** 11 Guanghua Rd.
*Tel: (010) 6532 1961.*
**USA** 3 Xiushiu Bei St.
*Tel: (010) 6532 3831.*

## Emergency Telephone Numbers
**Accidents/ambulance** *120.*
**Police** *110.*

## Hospitals
### BEIJING
**Capital Hospital/Peking Union Medical Hospital** (Foreigners' Emergency Clinic): *6th Fl, 53 Dongdanbei Ave.*
*Tel: (010) 6529 5269/5284.*

### GUANGZHOU (Canton)
**First Municipal Hospital,** 602 Renmin Bei Rd. *Tel: (020) 333 090.*

### SHANGHAI
**Shanghai No 1 Hospital,** 410 Suzhou Bei Rd. *Tel: (021) 6324 0090.*

## Thomas Cook
The Thomas Cook Worldwide Customer Promise offers free emergency assistance at any Thomas Cook Network location to travellers who have purchased their tickets at a Thomas Cook Network location. MasterCard cardholders may use any Thomas Cook Network location to report loss or theft of their card, and obtain an emergency card replacement, as a free service under the Thomas Cook MasterCard International Alliance. Use the Thomas Cook MasterCard Refund Centre (24-hour service) to report loss or theft within 24 hours (*tel: (441) 733 318 950*). In Beijing, Thomas Cook can be contacted at Room 0807, Beijing Tourism Tower, Jianguomenwai Street, Beijing (*tel: (010) 515 8193/8444 ext 2811*). In Hong Kong: Room 602, Tern Plaza, 5 Cameron Rd, Tsim Sha Tsui, Kowloon (*tel: (0852) 2853 9933*).

## Etiquette
It takes a while for both the Chinese and foreigners to get used to each other. While few Chinese are familiar with people from other lands, they appreciate the fact that they are different. Their curiosity leads to a lot of staring, but the intent is harmless. Casual dress is acceptable in most non-formal situations.

## Health
It is recommended that travellers keep tetanus and polio vaccinations up to date, and be vaccinated against typhoid and hepatitis A. Precautions against malaria should be taken by those travelling to rural areas or making river trips. Observe food and water hygiene precautions: drink bottled water, and ensure that food is cleanly prepared.

## Hitch-hiking
Hitching a ride is virtually non-existent in China, although it is possible to strike deals with drivers, particularly if a payment is made.

## Insurance

Be sure to take out comprehensive travel insurance before you travel to China. Travel insurance policies can be purchased through the AA, branches of Thomas Cook, and most travel agents.

## Lost Property

Airports, railway stations, and the more important bus depots all have lost-property offices. You should report loss of goods to the police.

## Maps

Some maps and city plans are available free in China from offices of the CITS and CTS. Most have to be paid for, and are usually available from street traders at low cost and in bookshops. Hong Kong and Macao maps are issued free by tourist offices and some hotels.

## Media

The English-language newspaper the *China Daily* is mainly filled with favourable 'news' about how well China is solving its problems. *Newsweek, Time,* the *International Herald Tribune,* the *Wall Street Journal Asia,* and *Business Week* are all on sale in major hotels in Beijing, Shanghai, and Guangzhou, while CNN, and occasionally BBC World Service Television, is likewise available. Otherwise, anyone determined to keep up with world events should bring shortwave radio receivers.

English language publications are available free in some big cities. They generally contain listings and events information, useful for expats and travellers. They are available in bars, restaurants, and hotels in Beijing, Shanghai, and Guangzhou. Titles

## LANGUAGE

Few Chinese speak English, although young people are learning fast.

The country's common language, *putonghua*, can be a minefield, even for basic tourist phrases, because incorrect tonal pronunciation gives words a completely different meaning to that intended. Most visitors find that sign language and gestures can take one a long way.

### TONE SYMBOLS

- ¯ 1st tone: high and level
- ´ 2nd tone: starting low and rising
- ˇ 3rd tone: starting low, falling, then rising
- ` 4th tone: starting high and falling

### NUMBERS

| | | | |
|---|---|---|---|
| zero | líng | five | wǔ |
| one | yī | six | liù |
| two | èr | seven | qī |
| three | sān | eight | bā |
| four | sì | nine | jiǔ |
| | | ten | shí |

### USEFUL WORDS AND PHRASES

| | |
|---|---|
| hello | ní hǎo |
| goodbye | zàijiàn |
| please | qǐng |
| thank you | xièxie |
| yes | duì |
| no | bú duì |
| how much? | dūoshǎo qián? |
| excuse me | qǐng wèn |
| I'm sorry | duìbuqī |
| I don't understand | wǒ budǒng |
| today | jīntiān |
| tomorrow | míngtiān |

include: *Beijing City Weekend, Beijing Metro, Metrozine* (Shanghai), *Shanghai Talk,* and *That's Guangzhou.*

## Money Matters

The main unit of currency is the yuan (¥), which is divided into 10 jiao, and one jiao is divided into 10 fen, all three of which units are known collectively as renminbi (RMB), or 'the people's money'. Notes are issued in denominations of 100, 50, 10, 5, 2, and 1 yuan, and 1, 2, and 5 jiao. Coins are 1 yuan,

The Chinese are enthusiastic tourists in their own country: the Great Wall

and 5, 2, and 1 jiao. Hong Kong and Macao have their own currency. At the time of writing, the Hong Kong dollar (HK$) = 1.06 RMB; the Macao pataca (MOP) = 1 RMB.

### Credit Cards and Cheques

Credit cards are not widely accepted outside the major hotels and Friendship Stores. US dollar traveller's cheques are recommended instead, but are only accepted at official Foreign Exchange Counters, which can be found in the main tourist areas. The Bank of China also has counters in hotels, in Friendship Stores, and in major department stores and their branches. The exchange rates are centrally fixed, and do not vary from place to place.

Cash machines are widely available in Hong Kong and Macao, and are beginning to be installed in China.

### National Holidays

**1 January** New Year
**Late January/early February**
    Chinese New Year (2/3-day holiday)
**8 March** Women's Day
**1 May** Labour Day
**4 May** Youth Day
**1 June** Children's Day
**1 July** Communist Party Day
**1 August** People's Liberation Army Day
**1 October** National Day

### Opening Hours

Government offices and public institutions open from 8am or 9am until 5pm or 6pm, with a two-hour break at lunch. Sunday is usually the weekly closing day, although some banks and foreign exchange offices may open on

Sunday morning. Friendship Stores and major department stores open daily 9am–7pm. Private businesses, such as shops and restaurants, open from early in the morning until late in the evening, and even into the early hours.

### Organised Tours
Bus and boat tours can be organised at any China Travel Service or China International Travel Service office. In addition, there are private companies offering such tours, at least one of which will have an office in the major hotels.

### Pharmacies
Because many Western medicines are not available in China, you should take your own prescription drugs and a supply of minor medicaments. Non-prescription drugs may be available in the shopping centres of major hotels. The same applies to tampons, contraceptives, and nappies. For more serious problems, ask your hotel or guide for assistance with a doctor's visit, or a trip to the local hospital. In Beijing, diplomatic missions have their own medical arrangements, and usually offer advice to foreigners.

### Places of Worship
Beijing, Shanghai, Guangzhou, and some other cities have cathedrals or churches where Christian services are held, though usually in Chinese.

### Police
The police are known as the Public Security Bureau (PSB), and officers wear green uniforms with peaked caps, not dissimilar to the uniforms of the PLA (People's Liberation Army). They are generally, though not always, helpful to foreigners, but this may be made difficult by the language barrier. The Foreign Affairs Branch of the local PSB deals with foreigners, and is staffed with officials who speak English.

### Post
Main post offices are open 8am–6pm, and offer a wide range of postal services. Like many government-operated bodies in China, however, the postal service is overmanned and inefficient. Ordinary postal operations are best handled through your hotel, if possible; if not, a Chinese-speaking guide is essential to help deal with the post office system.

### Public Transport
#### By Air
Air services and airports have improved greatly in China over recent years, but they still have a way to go before they can be considered reliable and fully safe. Although the network of routes operated by the big, regionally based carriers is extensive, demand outweighs supply. Early reservation, through CITS or airline booking offices, is essential.

#### By Train
Trains remain the most popular mode for long-distance travel and over the past few years China has been investing heavily in new lines and high-speed trains. Soft-class sleeper is the best way to travel on two-, three-, and four-day journeys across China, for this ensures a bunk in a four-berth cabin, sheets and blankets, and a restaurant car. Hard-class sleeper involves far less comfort in

six-berth open compartments. Non-sleeper trains are not comfortable for overnight journeys, and hard-seat class can be noisy, crowded, and dirty, yet give an atmospheric glimpse of the real China. Soft-seat and sleeper reservations can be made through CTS and CITS offices or direct from stations (hotels can also arrange these, for a fee).

## Local Transport
### By Bus
Buses and minibuses are extremely cheap in cities, but are always very crowded, and it is difficult to work out their schedule complexities. Many cities have long boulevards, however, and it is relatively easy to work out where the bus must be going, and hop on or off for short to medium journeys.

### By Metro
Beijing has a fast and efficient (but not extensive) metro system, and Shanghai now has two metro lines. Hong Kong's MTR network is excellent.

### By Taxi
These are plentiful as a rule, and can be waved-down in the street. Hotel taxis are expensive compared with street cabs. In some cities there are endless arguments over fares and routes, and honest taxi drivers are few. Beijing, Shanghai, and Guangzhou (Canton) are reasonable in this respect, and problems can often be resolved if you appeal to a passing police officer for help.

## Senior Citizens
Older people are made welcome in China, on the assumption that they are likely to spend more than youthful backpackers with fat agendas and thin wallets. China's own senior citizens are accorded a respectful place in society that makes them the envy of their counterparts in the youth-worshipping cities of the West.

Travelling in China can be difficult, however, and theoretical respect rarely translates into practical concessions, such as reduced rates or reserved seats.

Signage is clear and prominent on the streets

Travelling with an organised tour makes everything far easier, of course.

**Student and Youth Travel**

Exchange students resident in China can get reductions on accommodation in student dormitories, travel, and so on, but little concession is given for back-packing Western youths. Nevertheless, if you have time to spare, and do not mind a little hardship in your transport and accommodation arrangements, China can be done very cheaply.

**Telephones**

Country code 86 (if phoning China from abroad, omit the first 0 in the area code). Area codes are:

**Beijing** *010*; **Chengde** *0314*; **Chengdu** *028*; **Chongqing** *0811*; **Guangzhou** *020*; **Guilin** *0773*; **Harbin** *0451*; **Hong Kong** *0852*; **Kowloon** *0852*; **Macao** *0852*; **Lhasa** *0891*; **Nanjing** *025*; **Shanghai** *021*; **Suzhou** *0512*; **Urumqi** *0991*; and **Xi'an** *029*.

To dial abroad: 00 + country code + area code (minus the initial 0) + subscriber number.

**Australia** *61*
**Ireland** *353*
**New Zealand** *64*
**South Africa** *27*
**UK** *44*
**USA** and **Canada** *1*
**Operator** *114* (local); *113* (long distance). For operator in other areas call: *area code + 114*.

**Telex, faxes and telegrams**

Most major hotels have business centres where these services are available.

Modern telephone booths

**Charges**

Public telephones accept two 5-fen coins, or ¥20 and ¥100 telecards, but these are rare: it's best to rely on hotels or restaurants.

International direct-dial calls can be made from card-operated telephones and from hotel rooms and business centres; operator-assisted and collect calls cost more. Calls from hotel rooms will cost more than the standard cost, but local calls may be free for the first 30 seconds.

**Time**

In time, as with much else in China, the entire country dances to Beijing's tune. The capital's time is Greenwich Mean Time (GMT) + 8 hours, and Eastern Daylight Time (EDT) + 13 hours. This puts it 8 hours ahead of London, 13 hours ahead of New York, and 2 hours behind Melbourne.

**Tipping**

Most Chinese do not expect tips – with the important and growing exception of all those working directly with tourists. In Hong Kong and Macao, tipping is more widespread.

## Toilets

Most public toilets are not very pleasant, and squatting in public over an open sluice is a fairly common way of relieving oneself. In any case, it is wise to take your own toilet paper or tissues, as these are rarely available.

Toilets in the bigger hotels and restaurants are usually good, and the squeamish would be well advised to wait for such opportunities. In Hong Kong, Macao, and Shanghai, toilets are up to Western standards.

## Tourist Offices

Getting local tourist information in China is not always easy, although the bigger cities and important tourist zones may have some hotel-based brochures or a local guidebook. Tourist information offices do not exist, and though local offices of the China Travel Service and the China International Travel Service may provide some such information, their primary role is selling tours.

### Main CITS/CTS Offices

**Beijing** CITS, 103 Fuxingmen Nei Ave. *Tel: (010) 6601 1122*; CTS, 8 Dongjiaominxiang. *Tel: (010) 6512 9933.*
**Guangzhou** CTS, 10 Qiaoguang Rd. *Tel: (020) 8668 1163.*
**Shanghai** CITS, 33 Zhongshan Rd. *Tel: (021) 6439 3615.*
**Xi'an** CITS, 32 Changan Rd. *Tel: (029) 526 1437.*
**Guilin** CITS, 14 Ronghu Bei Rd. *Tel: (0773) 223 518.*
**Hong Kong** New Mandarin Plaza, Tower A, 12th Fl, 14 Science Museum Rd, Tsim Sha Tsui. *Tel: (0852) 2732 5888*; 4th Floor CTS House, 78–83 Connaught Rd. *Tel: (0852) 2853 3888.*

### International Tourist Offices

Chinese tourist offices abroad offer an efficient service and useful information.
**London** *4 Glentworth St. Tel: (020) 7935 9427.*
**New York** Lincoln Building, 60 East 42nd St, Suite 3126, NY 10165. *Tel: (212) 867 0271.*
**Sydney** 11th Floor, 55 Clarence St, NSW 2000. *Tel: (02) 299 4057.*

**Useful Websites:** *cits.net; chinawindow.com; chinanow.com; chinatravel.com; chinavista.com; travelchinaguide.com*

## Travellers with Disabilities

Lack of facilities, difficulty of access, and overloaded transport make life hard for those with mobility problems.
For further information, contact:
**UK:** Royal Association for Disability and Rehabilitation (RADAR), 25 Mortimer St, London W1N 8AB. *Tel: (020) 7637 5400.*
**US:** Advancement of Travel for the Handicapped, 26 Court St, New York, NY11242. *Tel: (212) 447 7284.*

**ACKNOWLEDGEMENTS**
Thomas Cook wishes to thank the photographers, picture libraries, and other organisations for the loan of the photographs reproduced in this book, to whom copyright in the photographs belongs.

INGRID BOOZ MOREJOHN PICTURE WORKS 2, 4, 10, 22, 23, 24, 27b, 41, 43, 44a, 44b, 45a, 58, 62, 72b, 73a, 81, 90, 92, 96, 97, 98, 106a, 108, 109, 111, 114, 115, 118, 118a, 118b, 119b, 128a, 129, 132, 133, 134, 135, 136, 137, 139a, 140, 141, 142, 143, 145, 146, 146a, 146b, 147, 148, 151, 162a, 162b, 163b, 168, 169, 170, 171, 174, 175a, 175b, 177, 178, 187, 188, 189, back cover top centre & right; PADDY BOOZ PICTURE WORKS 93, 128b; NICK TAPSELL FFOTOGRAFF 4b, 9, 11, 20b, 21, 40, 56, 87, 121, 123, 161, 167a, 179; PATRICIA AITHIE FFOTOGRAFF 13, 31, 32b, 33, 37, 88, 152, 154, 155, 167b; EVA CADRIO FFOTOGRAFF 14b; MIKE GERRARD FFOTOGRAFF 126b, 166; NEIL SETCHFIELD 14, 15, 17a, 78; CHRISTINE PEMBERTON 14b, 17b, 18a, 19, 28, 29, 30, 32a, 50, 74, 75, 94, 95, 116, 120, 126a, 156a, 156b, 157, 158, 160, 176; PICTURES COLOUR LIBRARY 16, 34a, 34b, 55, 100, 101; NATURE PHOTOGRAPHERS 130b; OTTO PFISTER 131; MARY EVANS PICTURE LIBRARY 138a, 138b, 139b

The remaining pictures are held in the AA PHOTO LIBRARY and were taken by ALEX KOUPRIANOFF.

**FOR LABURNUM TECHNOLOGIES**
| | | | |
|---|---|---|---|
| **Design Director** | Alpana Khare | **Photo Editor** | Radhika Singh |
| **Series Director** | Razia Grover | **DTP Designers** | Neeraj Aggarwal, |
| **Editors** | Madhavi Singh, Rajeev Jairam, | | Harish Aggarwal |
| | Deepshika Singh | | |

Updating and additional research on this edition was done by Susan Lafferty.
Thanks to Marie Lorimer for the Index.